Southeast Alaska

ALASKA GEOGRAPHIC

Volume 20, Number 2

EDITOR
Penny Rennick

PRODUCTION DIRECTOR
Kathy Doogan

STAFF WRITER
L.J. Campbell

BUSINESS & CIRCULATION MANAGER
Kevin Kerns

CUSTOMER SERVICE REPRESENTATIVE
Patty Bliss

POSTMASTER: Send address changes to
ALASKA GEOGRAPHIC®
P.O. Box 93370
Anchorage, Alaska 99509-3370

ISBN: 1-56661-010-9 (paper); 1-56661-011-7 (hardback)

PRICE TO NON-MEMBERS THIS ISSUE: $19.95

COLOR SEPARATIONS BY: Graphic Chromatics

PRINTED BY: Hart Press

PRINTED IN U.S.A.

COVER: *This original corner post from the Cape Fox Tlingit Raven tribal house was brought to Saxman in the 1930s. (Steve McCutcheon)*

PREVIOUS PAGE: *This trail winds among coastal conifers on a small peninsula between Sitka Sound and the mouth of the Indian River, part of Sitka National Historical Park. (Matt Johnson)*

FACING PAGE: *Dick Stack's skiff rests among beach grasses at Loring, on Naha Bay north of Ketchikan. (Mary Ida Henrikson)*

BOARD OF DIRECTORS

Richard Carlson, Kathy Doogan, Penny Rennick

Robert A. Henning, *President Emeritus*

ALASKA GEOGRAPHIC® (ISSN 0361-1353) is published quarterly by The Alaska Geographic Society, 639 West International Airport Road, Unit 38, Anchorage, AK 99518. Second-class postage paid at Anchorage, Alaska, and additional mailing offices. Copyright © 1993 by The Alaska Geographic Society. All rights reserved. Registered trademark: Alaska Geographic, ISSN 0361-1353; Key title Alaska Geographic.

THE ALASKA GEOGRAPHIC SOCIETY is a non-profit organization exploring new frontiers of knowledge across the lands of the Polar Rim, putting the geography book back in the classroom, exploring new methods of teaching and learning—sharing in the excitement of discovery in man's wonderful new world north of 51°16′.

SOCIETY MEMBERS receive *ALASKA GEOGRAPHIC*®, a quality magazine that devotes each quarterly issue to monographic in-depth coverage of a northern geographic region or resource-oriented subject.

MEMBERSHIP in The Alaska Geographic Society costs $39 per year, $49 to non-U.S. addresses. ($31.20 of the $39 is for a one-year subscription to *ALASKA GEOGRAPHIC*®.) Order from The Alaska Geographic Society, P.O. Box 93370, Anchorage, AK 99509-3370; phone (907) 562-0164, fax (907) 562-0479.

SUBMITTING PHOTOGRAPHS: Please write for a list of upcoming topics or other specific photo needs and a copy of our editorial guidelines. We cannot be responsible for unsolicited submissions. Submissions not accompanied by sufficient postage for return by certified mail will be returned by regular mail.

CHANGE OF ADDRESS: The post office does not automatically forward *ALASKA GEOGRAPHIC*® when you move. To ensure continuous service, please notify us six weeks before moving. Send your new address, and, if possible, your membership number or a mailing label from a recent *ALASKA GEOGRAPHIC*® to: The Alaska Geographic Society, P.O. Box 93370, Anchorage, AK 99509-3370.

MAILING LISTS: We occasionally make our members' names and addresses available to carefully screened publications and companies whose products and activities may be of interest to you. If you prefer not to receive such mailings, please advise us, and include your mailing label (or your name and address if label is not available).

The Library of Congress has cataloged this serial publication as follows:

Alaska Geographic. v.1-
[Anchorage, Alaska Geographic Society] 1972-
v. ill. (part col.). 23 x 31 cm.
Quarterly
Official publication of The Alaska Geographic Society.
Key title: Alaska geographic, ISSN 0361-1353.

1. Alaska—Description and travel—1959-
—Periodicals. I. Alaska Geographic Society.

F901.A266 917.98′04′505 72-92087

Library of Congress 75[79112] MARC-S

ABOUT THIS ISSUE: Fifteen years ago *ALASKA GEOGRAPHIC*® produced one of its all-time best-sellers, *Southeast, Alaska's Panhandle.* Much has changed in Southeast since that time, and we thought a new issue on one of the state's most beautiful regions was needed. Staff writer L.J. Campbell visited Southeast in early 1993 and returned to write the basic text and the article on the Alaska Marine Highway for this issue. Editor Penny Rennick contributed the Glacier Bay sidebar. Anthropologists Chris Wooley and Dr. Madonna Moss prepared the review of early man in Southeast, and reporter Marilee Enge, born and raised in Petersburg, describes growing up in this Norwegian outpost on Mitkof Island. From Bruce H. Baker of Juneau comes the sidebar on old-growth forest habitat.

Thank you to Linda Mickle of the Alaska Marine Highway System for arranging ferry passage through Southeast, and to the officers and crews of the *LeConte*, *Aurora* and particularly the *Malaspina*. Thanks also to the many people on the ferries and in the region's towns who consented to interviews about life in Southeast. A number of people made a special effort to help with this issue. In Sitka, we appreciate the assistance of Peter Corey, curator of collections for Sheldon Jackson Museum; Tlingit weaver Teri Rofkar; and Larry Larsen, deputy harbor master; and Sandy Smith of the Alaska Raptor Rehabilitation Center. In Angoon we called on K.J. Metcalf. In Ketchikan we acknowledge the efforts of Jackie Voigt of the visitor's bureau; Mike Hill of ProMech Air for the flight to Yes Bay; and Jim Baichtal, with the U.S. Forest Service, for the slide show of caves on Prince of Wales Island. In Craig we thank Barbara Permenter, who showed L.J. around; and Dennis Parsons, mechanics Joe and Scott at the Chevron station, and Henry Julian of Hollis, who helped when L.J. had car troubles. In Juneau, we appreciate the assistance of Marilyn Hansen of the visitor's bureau, and Karen Hansen of Wings of Alaska for the flight over Mendenhall Glacier. In Haines, we thank Annette Smith with the visitor's bureau, and state park ranger Bill Zack who arranged for L.J.'s trip to the Chilkat Bald Eagle Preserve. We appreciate the help of Vikki Mata for information on Sealaska, the Native regional corporation for Southeast.

Contents

"Paradise of the Poets"

When traveling to Alaska along North America's western coast, the first region of the state to appear is Southeast.

This narrow, elongated paisley of islands and sheltered seawater passages was sculpted by glaciers 10,000 years ago, occupied by Tlingit and Haida Indians, and claimed by Russia as her North Pacific headquarters. It was Alaska's most populated region until World War II.

Today, Southeast still has glaciers, Indians and a touch of Russia in restored buildings and artifacts. It is home to Alaska's state capital, Juneau. Thousands of visitors each year cruise the waterways of its famed Inside Passage. Thick stands of ancient spruce, cedar and hemlock trees cover most of its land, and most of the trees and land belong to the federal government. Nearly half the region is protected wilderness, including Misty Fiords National Monument, Admiralty Island National Monument and Glacier Bay National Park.

Wildlife abounds. Humpback, killer, gray and minke whales. Porpoises, dolphins, seals, sea lions. Chinook, red, pink, coho and chum salmon. Puffins, marbled murrelets, auklets and murres. Wolves, mountain goats, elk and moose. Even the small and slow, ice worms and banana slugs. Brown bears and eagles live here in some of the country's densest concentrations, and they feed in world-famous aggregations on the region's salmon. More deer live in Southeast than people.

The region's few dozen remote communities are tucked into river valleys or perched on steep hillsides, always facing the sea. Though seemingly isolated in the vast maze of water and land, they are connected by mail, telephone, radio and satellite television. Skiffs, cruisers, tugs, barges, ships and a fleet of state ferries churn Southeast's water. Floatplanes buzz overhead. One of the biggest industries here is logging, mostly to supply the region's two pulp mills. Fishing, some mining, government and an explosion in tourism also fuel the economy.

Southeasterners have for many years liked to claim they have it all. But with most of the land in federal hands, much of what happens is shaped by society's values and prevailing national politics. Increasing conflicts about who gets what, and for what use, have people here wondering if all they have is enough.

THE LAND

On the big map of Alaska, Southeast hangs on the lower right-hand corner, tucked neatly against Canada. Sometimes it is called Alaska's Panhandle for its shape and location.

Southeast barely joins the rest of the state in the narrow recesses of Icy Bay. From there,

FACING PAGE: *Termination dust, the season's first snowfall, frosts Mount McGinnis (4,228 feet), the Mendenhall Towers and Mount Wrather (5,968 feet) from Auke Lake near Juneau. (Bruce H. Baker)*

it stretches south some 525 miles to Dixon Entrance. The international boundary with Canada wraps from the southern tip of Dall Island through Portland Canal, north along the peaks of the Coast Mountains, then west above Skagway and Haines to a pinch at Mount Fairweather. Then it extends north along the Saint Elias Range, the highest coastal mountains in the world.

A strip of mountainous mainland runs the region's length. Massive ice caps on these mountains produce large glaciers. One of the largest on the continent, Malaspina Glacier, is located in the region's ice-packed northern tip. Some of Southeast's glaciers funnel down to tidewater and burp housesized icebergs into fiords. Glaciers higher on the mountainsides gush silty meltwater streams and rivers to the sea. Most of the region's major rivers — the Alsek, Chilkat, Taku, Unuk, Stikine — originate in Canada. From its glaciers and abundant rainfall, Southeast has thousands of lakes, streams and rivers. The sound of water plays everywhere, gurgling up close and roaring in the distance like the dull static of white noise.

For all practical purposes, Southeast is a body of islands. More than 1,000 islands make up its Alexander Archipelago. They range from tiny rocky protrusions to large mountainous islands covered with forests. Prince of Wales Island, the biggest in Southeast, is the third largest island in the nation behind Hawaii and Kodiak. An extinct volcano, Mount Edgecumbe, is a landmark on Kruzof Island west of Sitka. It erupted about 9,000 years ago spreading ash throughout much of the region.

Weaving through the archipelago are the sounds, straits, channels and narrows of the Inside Passage. Many of these seaways are deep. Chatham Strait, the major waterway bisecting the archipelago, plunges to depths of 2,000 feet while many other fiords reach 400-feet deep. Others are less generous; the 21-mile Wrangell Narrows is only about 21-feet deep at low tide, and strong tides rushing in from both ends create additional navigational challenges. But for mariners who can read its waters, the Inside Passage provides a route through Southeast relatively protected from the often turbulent Pacific Ocean to the west.

The steep-sided fiords, glaciers, forested islands, coves, sea caves, tide pools and miles of coastline offer mind-numbing views. In 1879, naturalist John Muir sailed into Southeast. "Never before this had I been embosomed in scenery so hopelessly beyond description," he wrote. "Tracing shining ways through fiord and sound, past forests and waterfalls, islands and mountains and far azure headlands, it seems as if surely we must at length reach the very paradise of the poets, the abode of the blessed."

THE CLIMATE

In general, Southeast gets lots of rain and has mild summers and winters. The interaction of mountains and ocean give it this maritime climate.

Summer temperatures average in the mid-50s, although occasionally the mercury climbs into the high 80s. This southerly region of Alaska receives more year-round daylight that helps keep temperatures warmer. Southeast is also bathed by ocean currents, another moderating influence. The warm Japan current swings to within 40 miles of Southeast's outer islands, sometimes even closer, producing cloud banks, temperature changes and bringing unusual tropical fish into the archipelago.

Winter temperatures usually range in the low to mid-30s with alternating snow and rain. However in the northern part of Southeast, winter temperatures may plunge below zero for a week or more when taku winds whip off the glaciers. Winter snows generally melt after a few days at the lower elevations in the southern third of the region, although ice may remain on streets and sidewalks causing hazardous walking for days. In the mountains and around glaciers, yearly snowfall may pile up 200 inches or more deep.

Long, incessant rains and drizzles characterize Southeast. Storms are most frequent and precipitation is heaviest November through January. Most weather

---

The cool, moist climate of Southeast produces abundant rainfall, and, at higher elevations and in the northern reaches, abundant snowfall. A thick blanket of snow covers Spaulding Meadows on Auke Mountain overlooking Auke Bay and Favorite Channel near Juneau. (Bruce H. Baker)

systems blow off the ocean, dropping their loads when they slam against the mountains.

Much of Southeast averages more than 100 inches of precipitation, but some places have much less, some much more depending on their relation to the nearest mountains and water. Yearly precipitation ranges from virtual drought of 26 inches in Skagway to more than 300 inches above Little Port Walter in the higher elevations of southern Baranof Island. Most everyone in the wetter microclimates of Southeast tromps around in brown rubber boots with waffle soles, good on sloppy ground as well as wet boat decks. On good-weather days, they turn

their boots down to their ankles.

Bright, clear days are the exception in Southeast; the sun shines only about 15 percent of the time. A string of bright, clear days can, strangely enough, be problematic since many people depend on rain-filled cisterns for water.

LEFT: *A raft of logs is towed through the channel at Sitka on their way to the Japanese-owned Alaska Pulp Corp. mill at Silver Bay. The plant, the largest private employer in Sitka, produces dissolving pulp used to make rayon and cellophane. (Dan Evans)*

BELOW: *Snow doesn't lessen the enthusiasm Haines Elementary school children have for their playground. (Harry M. Walker)*

THE FOREST

Southeast's cool, moist conditions have produced lush forests, an extension of the old-growth rain-belt forests of the Pacific Northwest. Designated Tongass National Forest in 1907, this greenbelt covers more than 73 percent of the land in Southeast.

The forest starts at sea level and climbs to 3,000 feet in the southern part and to about 1,800 feet farther north in the Icy Strait area. Western hemlock and Sitka spruce dominate the forest in the south. The hardiest stands grow in association with limestone karsts, and many of these areas are honeycombed with caves and vertical shafts. The nation's deepest known cave, El Cap Pit, and the third deepest, Sinkhole, are located in the karsts of northern Prince of Wales Island. The relationship between these limestone formations and the forest ecology is just beginning to be explored.

As it extends northward, the forest favors western and mountain hemlock. Red cedar extends only to the northern shore of Frederick Sound, and Alaska yellow cedar is often found only as small trees in swamps or muskegs. Red alder grows along streams, on landslides and is one of the first species to revegetate timber clear-cuts. Black cottonwood is common to mainland river valleys. Pacific silver fir is expanding northward into Southeast and has reached Misty Fiords. The region's wetness prevents naturally occurring fires like those that sweep through Interior forests.

The dense forest is broken up by muskeg bogs, glacial outwash plains and marshlands

FACING PAGE: *Sealevel Creek runs through the Sealevel mining claims on the northeast shore of Thorne Arm on Revillagigedo Island. (Chip Porter)*

LEFT: *Each species of wildlife depends on the characteristics of old-growth forest in its own way. Salmon rely on bank and channel stability that comes with old-growth forest, and black bears, such as this skilled fisherman at Anan Creek, depend on salmon as a chief source of food. (John Warden)*

BELOW: *Cone-shaped clusters of red berries, broad leaves and stems protected by stickers alert hikers in Southeast to the healthful but also hazardous devil's club. In the same family as ginseng, devil's club can be brewed into a tea, or crushed to make a poultice to lessen the irritation caused by its stickers. (David Job)*

The Ancient Forest and Wildlife Habitat Requirements

By Bruce H. Baker

Editor's note: *Now a forest resource consultant and freelance writer, Bruce recently completed 11 years as deputy director of the Alaska Department of Fish and Game's Habitat Division. Prior to that he had spent 12 years working for the U.S. Forest Service.*

Southeast Alaska's old-growth forests are diverse and biologically productive systems that have taken hundreds of years to develop, and many wildlife species have, since the last glaciation, come to depend on various characteristics of these forests. This is a land where because of abundant precipitation, the occurrence of fire is rare and when it does occur, it is usually localized. In the absence of fire or other sudden and widespread tree mortality, the forest has developed a state of dynamic equilibrium in which it normally replenishes itself as individual trees or groups of trees. It is common for tree seedlings, monarchs several hundred years old, and trees of any age and size in between to grow on the same acre. The largest blocks of natural tree regeneration are usually associated with patches of trees blown over during wind storms.

Unlike forests of other states, Alaska's coastal old-growth forests also still support the same complexes of wildlife species that they did prior to Russian settlement, and each species has come to depend on the old-growth characteristics in its own way.

For example, Sitka black-tailed deer are near the northern extent of their range here. Biologists have found that during winters of exceptionally deep, fresh snow, deer require a combination of small openings where there is enough sunlight for winter food plants to flourish, and large spruce and hemlock that can intercept enough snow for the deer to move about. Biologists have also learned that it takes about 200 years for trees to become large enough to provide adequate snow interception during severe winters.

The U.S. Fish and Wildlife Service has estimated that there are 10,000 adult bald eagles and several thousand immature bald eagles living in Southeast. Most eagle nests here are built in large, old, storm-damaged Sitka spruce or western hemlock. Mountain goats often seek refuge in old-growth timber during periods of intense winter storms on alpine ridges. Riparian old-growth is important for furbearers such as otters and marten. Even the salmon populations that humans, eagles and bears depend on must have the bank and channel stability, pools and riffles, clean water and spawning gravel, and nutrient cycling that large, streamside old-growth provides.

Finally, Southeast's mainland and islands support widely distributed populations of wolves and brown bears, species that have not fared well in the wake of intense land development and human settlement elsewhere. To the extent that their prey rely on old-growth forest, so do wolves and brown bears. In addition, bears commonly occupy dens under large spruces or in large snags.

Biologists point out the lack of evidence that wildlife populations can be maintained at historic levels in second-growth forests that are themselves logged as early as 100 years following initial clear-cutting. This is an important consideration for forest managers to factor into decisions as they set their goals for the sustained yield of wood fiber and wildlife well into the next century.

Plants of many vintages make up the old-growth ecosystem. On Prince of Wales Island, large woody debris growing on more large woody debris supports habitat in salmon streams. (Bruce H. Baker)

in river valleys and deltas. Wildflowers splash color against a backdrop of varied greens.

Beneath and on the fringes of the towering conifers flourish shrubs like blueberry, huckleberry, rusty menziesia, a dwarf dogwood called bunchberry, and devil's club, a spiny member of the ginseng family. Moss and ferns cover the ground and lichens evocatively called "old man's beard" drape many trees. Within the mature coniferous forest are openings where trees have blown down. Sunlight shines through these openings to the forest floor, allowing the variety of vegetation necessary for wildlife to survive.

FOREST ANIMALS

Southeast's ubiquitous Sitka black-tailed deer spend much time in the forest. The dense and rank undergrowth gives them protection from their two chief natural enemies, wolf and bear. When danger passes, they browse the openings. In winter, the forest canopy catches the snow giving the deer easier access to forage.

About 250,000 deer live in Southeast, and they are abundant as far north as the mainland west of Lynn Canal. A small group of deer transplanted to islands near Yakutat has spread to the mainland, which with its heavier snows and colder temperatures mark the deer's northern limit in Southeast. Deer thrive on the "ABC" islands — Admiralty, Baranof and Chichagof — because these islands have no wolves.

Wolves prowl the mainland and the islands south of Frederick Sound. For reasons not entirely understood, they do not live on the ABC islands.

These islands instead are home to the enormous and sometimes fierce brown bear. About 6,000 brown bears live in Southeast, and the densest concentrations are on Admiralty Island. At one per square mile, Admiralty's brown bear population is rivaled only by that of Kodiak Island and Katmai National Park and neighboring Becharof National Wildlife Refuge on the Alaska Peninsula.

At two bear viewing areas — Pack Creek on Admiralty and Anan Creek in the Stikine River drainage near Wrangell — bears congregate to feed on salmon to build their fat reserves before winter. They also eat deer, berries and roots.

Black bears, the most abundant and widely distributed bear species in Southeast, number about 17,000. They are found throughout the region except, like wolves, on the ABC islands. The blue, or glacier, bear — a color phase of the black bear — is seen sometimes near Yakutat and Juneau.

Mountain goats naturally occur in the alpine zone of the mainland, and some of the continent's largest goat populations are found here browsing meadows and traversing steep, rocky outcrops. There are about 14,000 mountain goats in Southeast, including those transplanted to Baranof and Revillagigedo islands.

An attempt to populate Kruzof Island with Roosevelt elk failed in the 1920s, but a more recent effort on Etolin Island succeeded. A small group of elk was placed here in 1987,

A pine grosbeak feeds on mountain ash berries near Juneau. (Lynn Schooler)

with plans to open hunting when the herd reaches 250 animals. In 1993, Etolin's population numbered 75. They have swum north to Zarembo Island, south to the mainland's Cleveland Peninsula, and west across Clarence Strait to Prince of Wales Island. State biologists worry that the expanding elk may push out indigenous deer, since they compete for the same food.

Moose, numbering about 2,500, are found only in a few places in Southeast, mostly in the larger river drainages and the Yakutat Forelands. From the Stikine River valley, some moose have migrated onto Mitkof and Wrangell islands where clear-cuts from logging provide temporary habitat. Moose

from the Chilkat population have crossed the Endicott River valley into Glacier Bay.

One of the more unusual Southeast moose encounters happened in summer 1992. Two fishermen in a boat at the north end of Chichagof Island spotted a pair of moose swimming toward Glacier Bay. The men reported seeing killer whales attack the moose, killing one. The other moose escaped, but then got tangled in a kelp bed near shore and drowned.

Southeast hosts an assortment of smaller land mammals — lynx, wolverines, foxes, mink, land otters. Shrews, red squirrels, brown bats, flying squirrels, deer mice, red-backed voles, porcupines and marten dwell in the forest and adjacent habitats.

Blue grouse, great horned owls, woodpeckers, Steller's jays and thrushes are among the forest's feathered inhabitants. Robins, fox sparrows, hummingbirds and swallows are heard and seen along the forest edge. Vancouver Canada geese nest in the old-growth forest. More bald eagles live in Southeast than in any other place in the world. Admiralty Island supports the most nesting pairs, while the Chilkat River valley north of Haines draws thousands of eagles to feed in winter on late salmon runs.

THE SEA

The ocean and its complex coastlines, with rocky intertidal areas, mud flats and sandy beaches, support a world of invertebrates, fish, birds and sea mammals.

Some of the richest marine habitat occurs

Needlefish drape from the beak of this tufted puffin posing near its burrow. It can also crush the shells of mollusks and sea urchins with its strong bill. (John Hyde)

Visitors can see breaching humpback whales on many of Southeast's waterways. This view shows the ventral or under surface of the whale. When the humpback is feeding, the grooves expand to allow the whale to gulp great quantities of water into its mouth, where baleen plates hanging from its upper palate sift krill and small fish, the bulk of the whale's diet. (John Hyde)

at the mouths of Southeast's many rivers where salt and fresh waters mix, stirred by twice daily ocean tides. Southeast tides can fluctuate nearly 25 feet, from an extreme of minus 4.6 feet to plus 20 feet.

Invertebrates found in the region's waters include Dungeness, Tanner and king crab, shrimp, butter clams, sea urchins and sea cucumbers. The most significant fish in Southeast is the Pacific salmon. Each year during summer and fall five species — sockeye, chum, chinook, coho and pink — return by the thousands to spawn in the region's rivers and streams. Herring, halibut and sablefish, or black cod, along with Pacific perch, walleye pollock and rockfish are other commercially important fish. More than 100 species of fish and sea creatures common to Southeast waters can easily be seen swimming in aquariums of the visitor's center at the Gastineau Salmon Hatchery in Juneau.

Several species of marine mammals, such as Dall and harbor porpoises and humpback, fin and Pacific killer whales, are common in Southeast waters. Gray whales and northern fur seals pass offshore during migration, and the elephant seal has been recorded on occasion. Steller sea lions, although considered threatened because of declines elsewhere, are stable and increasing in numbers in Southeast. The sea lion rookery complex near Forrester Island is the largest in the world. Sea

otters, almost hunted to extinction in the early American period, are making a comeback and are hunted by Natives.

Large numbers of waterfowl, such as diving ducks, mallards, mergansers and Canada geese, flock here and more than 50 species of seabirds, including terns, gulls, cormorants, auklets and murres, have been sighted in the coastal waters of the region. Forrester, Hazy and Saint Lazaria islands on the outer coast are part of the National Wildlife Refuge system because of their numbers of nesting seabirds.

HISTORY

Southeast's history reaches back to its earliest inhabitants whose descendants became the region's modern Native peoples

— Tlingit, Haida and Tsimshian Indians. They explored, hunted, fished and claimed the lands and waters as glaciers began receding some 10,000 years ago. Evidence uncovered recently in caves on Prince of Wales Island indicates that the fringes of the outer islands may have escaped glaciation.

The land and ocean supplied them with an abundance of food and materials for shelter and tools, and they developed a rich, sophisticated culture. Obvious evidence of this Native heritage appears throughout Southeast today in carved totem poles, silver work and dance regalia.

Russians came to Southeast chasing the fur-bearing sea mammals, primarily sea otters. Despite fierce attacks by the Tlingits, the Russians built and rebuilt Sitka, called by

LEFT: *Euphausiids, shrimplike crustaceans about 1 inch long and generally known as krill, are trapped at low tide along Wrangell Narrows. (Don Cornelius)*

ABOVE: *A quillback rockfish, prized in restaurants in the Orient where it is steamed whole, swims near a sea urchin in shallow waters in Southeast. (Art Sutch)*

some the "capital of the Pacific." Russia's sale of Alaska to the United States in 1867 was formalized in ceremony here. The allure of Southeast was experienced as well by English, Spanish and French explorers who left their names behind. Canada even tried to extend its claims to tidewater during boundary settlements at the turn of the century.

In the early American period, the fur trade remained as the main economic interest until the fur-bearing animals were practically wiped out. Foxes were introduced on Southeast islands, but they did not survive. It was salmon that attracted entrepreneurs and renewed interest in the land known as Seward's Folly. Salmon were present in such

large numbers that it was rumored streams could be crossed by walking on their backs.

Numerous canneries sprung up after the first were established at Klawock and Old Sitka in 1878. Some of the region's earliest logging and sawmills came from the need for wood to build packing crates for canned salmon. The size of the salmon pack rapidly increased until it peaked in the late 1930s, when runs began to decline.

Minerals spurred some of Southeast's biggest population surges. Discoveries of gold in Southeast shortly after the purchase of Alaska brought some of the first pioneers, and they set up the first full-fledged gold mining camp, Shuck Camp, near Windham Bay. The Stikine River became a popular route to gold

fields of the Cassiar District of British Columbia in the 1870s. Prospectors spread from the Stikine and Cassiar districts into the Alexander Archipelago and neighboring mainland. Gold was discovered in 1880 at what is now Juneau, and in 1881 at Douglas across Gastineau Channel.

With this concentration of mining and the resulting increase in people, the territorial capital moved from Sitka to Juneau in 1906. Southeast became the dominant region of Alaska, a position it held until World War II when military activity and the Alaska Highway shifted emphasis to Anchorage and Fairbanks. The war also halted major gold operations.

The basic economy in Southeast began to change midcentury with the development of large-scale logging. Pulp mills at Ketchikan and Sitka opened. Sawmills were expanded to export cants to Japan and lumber to domestic markets in the contiguous United States.

THE ECONOMY

Natural resources — sea animals, mineral and forest products — traditionally have been the mainstay of Southeast's economy. Fishing continues to be vitally important to many people, who own boats or work on fishing crews. Seafood processing and the timber industry employ one of every six Southeast residents. Government, the region's largest employer, reigns in Juneau, the state capital and the state's third largest city. Tourism is booming throughout the region.

The timber industry supplies jobs in pulp mills, sawmills, logging and numerous support services. It is the economic backbone for much of Southeast and it is increasingly under pressure. Most of the logging in Tongass National Forest is done to supply pulp mills in Ketchikan and Sitka, the largest private employers in those towns. These mills

opened in the 1950s as part of a federal effort to provide a long-term economy in Southeast. The government promised to supply the mills with timber for 50 years. The contracts end in the years 2004 and 2011.

Critics of Tongass logging seek changes that cloud the future of the industry in Southeast. Meanwhile, the pulp mills face possibly stricter air and water standards that may force costly upgrades in pollution control equipment.

The salmon seiner Odyssey *plies the waters of Chomondeley Sound on Prince of Wales Island's eastern shore. Fishermen in Southeast earned more than $92 million from their salmon catch in 1992. (Chip Porter)*

ABOVE: *A rock arch marks the southwest end of George Island off the northwest tip of Chichagof Island in Cross Sound. (Chip Porter)*

LEFT: *Marcia Imers feeds salmon fry at Takatz Bay on the east side of Baranof Island. (Dan Evans)*

are sold under contract to the pulp mills. Some of the service's own wildlife biologists contend that the widespread practice of clear-cutting Tongass' old-growth threatens survival of certain animal species, and they recommend reducing harvests 25 percent. Some foresters, on the other hand, say the forest could support even higher harvest levels.

Responding to pressure from conservation groups seeking protection of old-growth, Congress in 1990 withdrew a million acres of the forest for wilderness and roadless areas. Added to the wilderness areas established in 1980 by the Alaska National Interest Lands Conservation Act, there are now about 6.5 million acres of Tongass off limits to logging — a mix of ice, alpine and forests. The forest service maintains that of the 9.5 million timbered acres in Tongass, only 5.5 million acres are commercially harvestable, including some in the wilderness areas.

Since 1954, less than 400,000 acres of the forest old-growth has been logged, according to the forest service, and by the end of a 100-year cycle, only 20 percent of the old-growth will have been taken. The forest service timber managers say this poses no threat to wildlife. Conservationists, on the other hand, contend that the most commercially important old-growth, which makes up the smallest percentage of the total forest, also provides the most important wildlife habitat, and is the part of the forest disappearing at the fastest rate.

Native groups, collectively the second largest landowners in Southeast, log their lands also. Most of their logs are exported in rounds to Asia, with some sold to the pulp mills. First-growth harvests on Native lands, at about 100 million board feet a year in 1992, are projected to end within the decade. Second-growth timber stands take 60 to 120 years to reach harvest size, although thinning

In 1993, the U.S. Forest Service was revising its plans for managing the 16.9-million-acre Tongass. Among other things, the forest service was trying to set timber harvests to meet its pulp mill contracts and protect wildlife numbers. The forest service proposes harvesting 418 million board feet a year, of which 271 million board feet a year

A favorite getaway for Ketchikan residents is nearby Ward Lake Recreation Area. (Chip Porter)

of those stands during the first 20 years of growth will produce some pulp timber. When second-growth timber reaches maturity, the industry will likely move from pulp production toward manufacture of products like wafer and particle board.

Sealaska, the regional corporation established in 1971 by the Alaska Native Claims Settlement Act to represent Southeast Natives, owns 340,000 acres of timber and about 600,000 subsurface acres. The 10 village and two urban Native corporations under ANCSA were allotted a total of about 286,400 acres.

Fishing in Southeast continues to provide a traditional way of life. Villages in coastal areas depend on income from fish harvests and seasonal processing.

Salmon leads the commercial fisheries of Southeast in importance, both in number of people involved and value of the catch. More than 28 percent of the salmon caught in Alaska in 1992 came out of Southeast, the leading producer in numbers of fish and slightly behind Bristol Bay in poundage. Southeast produces far more pinks, also more chinook, coho and chums, than any other region. The ex-vessel value, the price paid to fishermen, of Southeast's salmon fishery exceeded $92 million in 1992.

Most commercial fishermen catch salmon with purse seines and gillnets, although a number use power trolls and a few troll by hand. Getting into the limited entry salmon fishery is not cheap. A Southeast gillnet permit goes for about $75,500 while seine permits sell for $65,000 when they are available.

To rebuild depleted runs that reached all-time lows in the late 1950s and early 1960s, a hatchery program was started in Southeast in 1971. Today, 16 private non-profit hatcheries and four state-operated hatcheries enhance runs for both commercial and sport fishermen. New salmon products being developed in Southeast include breaded salmon nuggets, salmon ham and microwaveable salmon cans.

Other commercial fisheries in Southeast include: significant takes of halibut and black cod; lucrative sac-roe and spawn-on-kelp herring fisheries; small harvests of crab; longlining for rockfish and Pacific cod; oyster farming; and a growing fishery for sea urchins, sea cucumbers, scallops and com-

Low light illuminates Mendenhall lake and glacier and peaks of the Coast Range. The lake and glacier commemorate Professor Thomas Corwin Mendenhall (1841-1924), a former superintendent of the U.S. Coast & Geodetic Survey. (John Hyde)

mercial clams called geoducks (gooy-ducks). In 1993, a federal groundfish fisheries commission instituted a controversial quota system for halibut and black cod fishermen based on their past participation and catch in the fishery.

Mining plays a low-key role in the region's economy. Prospecting and exploration continues sporadically for gold, as well as silver, copper, lead, zinc, molybdenum, palladium and industrial minerals like marble, limestone and gypsum.

The largest silver producer in the world operated at Greens Creek on Admiralty Island from 1989 until April 1993. Low metal prices triggered its sudden closure, putting nearly 250 people in the Juneau area out of work. The loss of these high-paying jobs, average salary of $50,000 a year, sent shock waves through Southeast. Kennecott Corp., the mine's operator and majority owner, predicted the mine would not reopen for at least two years. Small amounts of gold, lead and zinc were also produced at Greens Creek.

The failure of Greens Creek cast uncertainty on other pending mineral ventures. In early 1993, Echo Bay Mines was in the permitting process to reopen two historic mines in the Juneau area — the Alaska-Juneau (A-J) gold mine near downtown and the Kensington mine in Berner's Bay. The company's efforts were being met with resistance from environmental groups. Elsewhere in Southeast, mining giant Cominco, Toronto-based LAC Minerals and Sealaska Corp. are

prospecting marble, copper and limestone deposits. Cominco also holds the world's largest known molybdenum deposit, located inside Misty Fiords National Monument near Ketchikan. Offshore from Yakutat, an oil and gas lease sale tentatively is scheduled for mid-1995. Wells drilled in the area in the late 1970s are plugged and abandoned.

Canadian mining stimulates the economies of several Southeast towns. Lead concentrate from Yukon Territory mines is shipped out of Skagway. Gold ore from Cominco's Snip mine in British Columbia comes through Wrangell. Controversial plans to develop the Windy Craggy zinc deposit in B.C. include bringing ore through Haines.

Government provides a significant number of jobs throughout the region with the state ferry system, schools, the postal service and U.S. Forest Service. Government accounts for half of all jobs in Juneau. The U.S. Coast Guard operates its main Southeast base in Ketchikan, employing about 200 people. This base is responsible for enforcement of fishing regulations and coordinating search and rescue operations for the entire region. The Ketchikan base is assisted by a station in Juneau and an air station in Sitka.

Tourism and recreation are major components of the region's economy. The glaciers, mountains, sheltered waterways, wild lands and fish and wildlife provide recreational opportunities that often cannot be experienced elsewhere in the United States.

Cruise ships bring 200,000 to 300,000 visitors into Southeast each summer. Sometimes five ships will dock at once in places like Ketchikan, Juneau and Skagway, flooding downtown streets with as many as 5,000 people. Southeast businesses cater to tourists, but locals tire of the crowds and clogged streets. A downtown errand that might

Near Sitka, the seiner Miss Susan *makes a set in the multimillion-dollar herring roe fishery. (Ernest Manewal)*

normally take 10 minutes can take hours when cruise ships are in town. Southeast towns are grappling with how handle the growing number of visitors, given limits in land and money to expand roads, campgrounds and other public facilities. Tour operators predict two to three times more cruise ships plying Southeast's waterways by the year 2000.

Southeast is beginning to get a share of the relatively new business of ecotourism, which targets mostly visitors wanting low-impact wilderness adventures. For instance, small cruise ships provide kayaks and guides so clients can explore shorelines up close. Local outfitters, who in the past have concentrated on fishing and hunting charters, are beginning to tap the market for wilderness sightseeing as well.

Trails from salt water to inland lakes and along rivers and steams provide access to cut-throat, rainbow, Dolly Varden, steelhead and other sport fish species. The U.S. Forest Service rents nearly 150 cabins throughout the region. World-class wilderness lodges operate in Southeast, and several towns compete for bragging rights to the best chinook salmon and halibut fishing. Boat charter businesses and floatplane companies cater to sport hunters and fishermen and sightseers. Boating, beachcombing, fishing, hunting, hiking, caving, surfing and photography are other recreational pursuits for locals and visitors alike.

THE PEOPLE

A feeling of vastness, wilderness and solitude is imparted and reinforced by the low-population density of Southeast. At least 95 percent of the land in Southeast is federal. Little of the land is occupied; much cannot be. Only 69,000 people live in Southeast, according to the 1990 federal census. Juneau is the largest town, with about 29,000 people. More than 91 percent of the region's people live in the five major urban areas of Juneau, Sitka, Ketchikan, Petersburg and Wrangell. Most of the others live in some 40 smaller settlements and logging camps, some as small as the communities of Kasaan, 54, and Kupreanof, 23.

Natives — mostly Tlingits — account for about 20 percent of the population. Many of the Tlingit, Haida and Tsimshian people live in urban Southeast, although some have chosen to remain in their traditional villages. Tlingit strongholds include Angoon, Hoonah, Saxman, Kasaan, Kake, Klawock, Klukwan and Yakutat. Hydaburg is considered a Haida village, while Metlakatla —the only Indian reservation in Alaska — is the Tsimshian traditional home.

For the most part, Southeast's communities are not connected by road. Most people travel by boat or airplane. The Alaska Marine Highway with its fleet of ferries provides regularly scheduled public transportation throughout the region.

These communities began in a variety of ways. Some were settled before the white man arrived, many attribute their founding to the mighty salmon, and a few can look back to the glitter of gold.

Ten Thousand Years of Human History in Southeast

By Chris Wooley and Madonna Moss

Editor's note: *Anthropologist Chris Wooley, who specializes in coastal archaeology, has 10 years experience exploring the history of ancient man in Alaska. Dr. Madonna Moss is assistant professor of anthropology at the University of Oregon with extensive experience in Southeast Alaska.*

There are many different ways to preserve the past. The oral traditions of Southeast Alaska's Tlingit people contain a detailed record of Tlingit history, starting with the moment Raven created the first people. Each of the many Tlingit clans have their own accounts describing migrations to their ancestral hunting grounds, fishing places and gathering areas. Territories shifted as clans grew. As a clan flourished, some members set off to settle other areas. Oral traditions also preserve genealogies, record social alliances, and describe how certain clans obtained their right to use animal crests and other inherited privileges. Much of this knowledge continues to be passed on through the ancient and sophisticated art of Tlingit oratory. Many students and scholars like Nora and Richard Dauenhauer of the Sealaska Heritage Foundation have recorded Tlingit history and oral literature on audio tapes and in books.

Unfortunately, huge chunks of Tlingit oral history have probably been lost. Starting in the late 1700s and continuing into the 1800s, many Tlingit people died from epidemic diseases introduced by EuroAmerican explorers, traders and colonists. Because only selected clan representatives have the right to speak about the history of their clan, when these people died their knowledge was lost and can never be fully restored. However, other aspects of Southeast Alaska's human history can be reconstructed by examining the legacy that has survived on the landscape.

Although Tlingit culture has been influenced by EuroAmerican customs and disease for more than 200 years, the culture endures because the Tlingit have adapted. The subsistence lifestyle persists in many villages alongside the administration of Tlingit owned and managed corporations. Clan affiliation is still central to Tlingit identity, and memorial potlatches persist as an important institution. Oral traditions and history contain strong evidence for the dynamic nature of Tlingit culture and society, a trait evident in the archaeological record as well.

Southeast Alaska contains many different types of marine and terrestrial habitat. The region has undergone many episodes of

FACING PAGE: *For centuries Natives of Southeast have gathered seaweed and shellfish in tidal pools, such as this one protected by a basalt arch on St. Lazaria Island. They cooked seaweed into a soup, gathered blue mussels and small clams to eat, and put kelp leaves in the bottom of baskets when they were used for cooking. (John Hyde)*

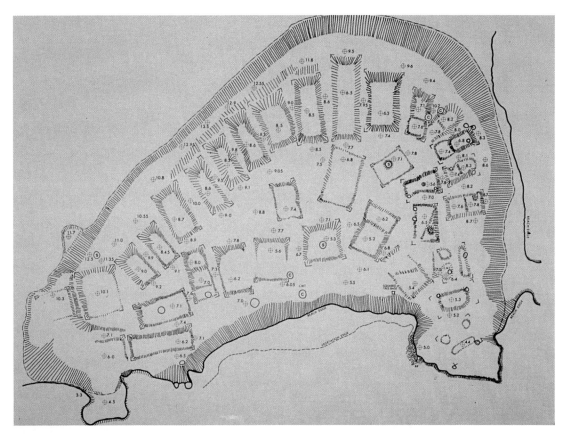

8,000-year-old artifacts from Chuck Lake on Heceta Island and from Thorne River on Prince of Wales Island demonstrate that Native people have been harvesting marine resources for a long time. Through the millennia, Southeast coastal cultures developed extremely effective hunting and fishing technologies and achieved a high degree of social complexity.

Although the period between 4,000 and 6,500 years ago is virtually unknown, some of the basic features of Tlingit life were established by about 3,500 years ago. People lived in large plank houses in villages occupied nearly all year around. Hair seals, fur seals, dolphins and sea lions were harpooned from large cedar canoes. These kills supplied important meat and fat, as did land mammals including deer, bears and mountain goats. Bottomfish and salmon were caught with carved wood and bone hooks attached to lines made of spruce root. Groups cooperated in gathering enormous amounts of salmon with traps and weirs, and caught other inshore schooling fish such as herring with traps and rakes. Waterfowl of all types were hunted and snared, and their eggs were collected from rookeries. Berries, seaweed, tree bark and other staples, including many usable items beached by the tide, were collected by clan members from distinct clan territories.

For thousands of years before Euro-American contact, Natives traded exotic materials throughout Southeast and adjacent

climate change, and human groups have successfully adapted to these environmental shifts and to the area's diverse resources. Some Native groups migrated into and out of the region, while other groups may have resided in the area for a long period of time. Tlingit origins include populations that moved into coastal Southeast from the interior via rivers like the Stikine and Taku, and from offshore islands near Prince Rupert, British Columbia. For example, a major Tlingit village on the British Columbia side of Dixon Entrance once accommodated more than 600 people in 35 large communal houses. This complex and ancient village was

abandoned about A.D. 1650 — before direct EuroAmerican contact. It is not clear why the people left, but those who moved from this village across Dixon Entrance and settled in southern Southeast were among the ancestors of modern Tlingit people. About this same time the ancestors of modern Haida also moved into southern Southeast from the Queen Charlottle Islands farther off the British Columbia coast.

The most ancient evidence for human occupation and use of Southeast is almost 10,000 years old. Stone tools from Hidden Falls on Baranof Island and Ground Hog Bay on the Chilkat Peninsula, as well as 7,000- to

regions. Obsidian (volcanic glass), boxes of eulachon oil (rendered from smeltlike candle-fish) and strings of dentalia shells were traded through sophisticated networks long before the arrival of EuroAmerican traders. Native people were so successful at living on the coast that populations grew quite dense. Around 1,500 years ago, competition for access to food resources grew fierce and conflicts erupted. Fortified village sites began to emerge about that time, indicating wide-spread friction. Tlingit warriors used distinc-tive combat equipment including slat armor made of wooden or sea mammal bone slats laced together, helmets and war clubs during raids and skirmishes. Captives taken during these conflicts were considered clan property and worked as laborers.

History is marked on the Southeast landscape in many ways. Rock carvings (petroglyphs) and rock paintings (pictographs) often contain crest designs that marked clan territories or commemorated important mythological and historical events. Many of the region's popular beaches and favorite fishing spots are places where the Tlingit established villages and camps. Some places still retain signs of recent Tlingit occupation with their collapsing smokehouses and furrowed rows from gardening potatoes. Research has shown that some of these historic sites are located on top of even older settlements dating to the time before EuroAmerican contact in 1741. Land and resource development in the region poses both problems and opportunities for preserving archaeological sites since proposed developments often have the potential to affect archaeological ruins or other sites of cultural significance protected by law.

In addition to the physical remains of archaeological sites, history is also documented in Tlingit place names. Although many of these probably have been lost, a remarkable number have survived and help tell the history of the Tlingit people and their close ties to the land. Names of particular bays might commemorate individuals lost in an important battle or canoe accident, or a place name may relate how a clan obtained the right to use a particular crest animal, such as a raven, bear, wolf, sea lion, killer whale or dogfish (shark). Other place names recount why places were originally settled or why they were abandoned. Landmarks like unusual rock formations are often named and associated with stories of Raven.

No episode of culture change was as de-structive as the initial phase of EuroAmerican contact (1741 to 1820). During this period, disease epidemics, warfare and migrations annihilated many local groups and their narrative histories. Groups who were able to control the fur trade by hunting or trading for sea otter pelts did so at the expense of harvesting other traditional foods. The spread of disease and violent competition among the Tlingits and their neighbors for access to trading ships and for valuable sea otter, beaver and land otter furs resulted in even further havoc. The loss of local knowledge and the adjustment to a new way of life

Anne Sudkamp holds an obsidian microblade core uncovered at the Thorne River archaeological site on Prince of Wales Island. (Don Pitcher)

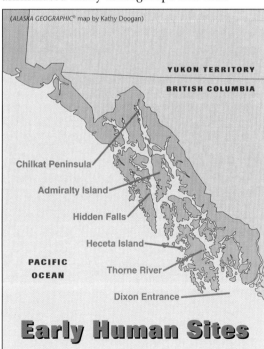

(ALASKA GEOGRAPHIC® map by Kathy Doogan)

YUKON TERRITORY

BRITISH COLUMBIA

Chilkat Peninsula

Admiralty Island

Hidden Falls

Heceta Island

PACIFIC OCEAN

Thorne River

Dixon Entrance

Early Human Sites

during this era may help explain why some aspects of the Native history of Southeast are poorly understood today.

Many historians and students of Native culture assume that the Tlingit who lived in Southeast before EuroAmerican contact followed a seasonal round of fish and game harvesting. According to this model, large groups of people lived in villages of permanent communal houses during the winter. In the spring, summer and fall the people split up into smaller groups and moved to temporary outlying camps where resources were harvested and preserved. The groups reassembled at winter villages for ceremonials in late fall.

Seasonal changes in residence were customary for Tlingit groups during the 1800s, but they were probably uncommon before EuroAmericans arrived. By the mid-1800s, the Tlingit population had declined to the point where remnants of many formerly large groups abandoned nearly vacant villages and consolidated at the remaining viable villages. Because of the distances between the still-viable villages and the resource areas of abandoned villages, old resource areas could only be used productively on a seasonal basis. Seasonal camps were set up at these resource areas, and seasonal movements became the most efficient way to fish, hunt and gather in territories that had lost the majority of their year-round human population. New economic pressures also began to influence the seasonal movements and subsistence schemes of the Tlingit. Seasonal movements probably were not as pronounced before EuroAmerican contact because populations were more dense and one group's resource territory typically bordered on the territory of another. A "seasonal round" was not an ideal strategy for dense populations of maritime people dependent on a wide variety of sea mammals, fish and shellfish — resources that generally were available in all seasons from a single site inhabited by talented hunters, gatherers and processors.

Issues such as the seasonal use of village sites, the growth of cooperative subsistence

BELOW: *This sharpened, wooden stake from a fishing weir is well-preserved because it was buried in intertidal mud flats. Several radiocarbon dated weirs in Southeast are more than 3,000 years old. (Dr. Madonna Moss)*

RIGHT: *Early Native people on Wrangell Island carved these petroglyphs in some of the boulders lining the beach between the airport and city center at Wrangell. Some petroglyphs marked boundaries of clan territories; others noted important mythological or historical events. (John Hyde)*

ABOVE: *This island is the site of a Tlingit fort near Admiralty Island known as Daux Hoat Kanadaa, "Where the tide passes back and forth." Swirling tidal currents around the island fort enhanced its defensibility. (Dr. Madonna Moss)*

RIGHT: *With the sponsorship of Sealaska Corp. and the Alaska State Museum, archaeologists Bob Betts (left) and Jon Loring excavate this fish trap, estimated to be about 700 years old, near the confluence of Montana Creek and the Mendenhall River in fall 1991. (David Job)*

schemes, the use of forts and the origins and development of Tlingit traditions remain to be analyzed. For precise analysis, hundreds of square miles of Southeast coastline need to be examined for evidence of past human use, with the lessons of the oral traditions in mind. Respect for the original residents of Southeast, their contemporary descendants and their traditions is necessary to understand the region's history. There are many ways to document history, and there are even more ways to transmit historical knowledge. Southeast Alaska's history will become clearer as research by Tlingit and non-Tlingit people proceeds.

The Alaska Marine Highway

Southeast Alaska is a place of boats and floatplanes. Most people live in small towns on the fringe of islands, separated from the rest of the world by miles of ocean, mountains and forests, and they travel by air or water. Every community in Southeast has some roads, but few communities connect that way. Only in Haines, Skagway and tiny Hyder do local roads lead outside to the larger, continental road network.

Yet, one of the most unusual highways in America runs along the Southeast coast. Thousands of people and vehicles each year travel this federally funded expressway. This is the Alaska Marine Highway, an important thoroughfare linking Southeast communities with each other and their mainland cousins.

A fleet of eight blue and white ferries regularly travel this marine highway. Three of them serve Prince William Sound to the Aleutian Islands, in southcentral and southwestern Alaska. The other five sail Southeast. The three largest of these —

Columbia, Matanuska and *Malaspina* — sail the length of the route, 1,080 miles from Skagway on the north to Bellingham, Wash., on the south. The two smaller vessels — *Aurora* and *LeConte* — make shorter jogs between outlying communities within Southeast.

The ferries share Southeast's Inside Passage with cruise liners, trollers, seiners, cabin cruisers, sailboats, freight barges, tugs and Asian log ships. But unlike the other vessels, they stop several times each week in 28 of the region's communities, as well as Prince Rupert, British Columbia, and Bellingham. All descriptions of people and conveyances come aboard: families, tourists, fishermen, loggers, cars, trucks, refrigerated vans of groceries, bikes, skiffs, even trailers of circus animals. Ferries take a while to get where they are going, but the fares are relatively cheap and the service dependable, an important alternative in a place where flying is pricey and the weather often dicey.

■ ■ ■

New Year's Day, 1993. The 235-foot *LeConte* is taking on passengers at Juneau for a 17-hour voyage to Sitka with stops at Hoonah, Tenakee Springs and Angoon. Passengers with vehicles drive down a ramp of steel grating onto the ship's car deck. They park in tight rows, motioned into place by a few crewmen bundled against the wet cold in insulated overalls. Other passengers, some carrying duffels and suitcases, walk down the ramp and follow a yellow-painted crosswalk between the cars to an interior flight of stairs that lead up to a small lobby on the main deck.

FACING PAGE: *One of Alaska's smaller ferries, the* LeConte, *is tied up at the dock at Sitka. Within a short walk is the site of Old Sitka, location of the original Russian settlement of St. Michael's Redoubt that was attacked by Tlingits in June 1802. (Harold Wahlman)*

About 180 passengers crowd the ship, milling around the main passenger deck. The forward half of this deck is a large carpeted lounge of reclining chairs enclosed by huge glass windows that overlook the bow of the ship for a panorama of oncoming scenery. A smaller side lounge, cafeteria, dining room and bar make up the rest of the deck. The larger ferries have more passenger decks with additional lounges, bars and work rooms of tables and chairs, along with staterooms that can sleep 250 to 300 people. But on the *LeConte*, most people sleep in chairs. Several families with small children have spread out sleeping bags, books and toys on the floor beneath their seats.

A few hardy passengers traipse up another flight of stairs to the open-air observation deck facing the stern. They pile their belongings on chaise lounges in a partially enclosed area at midship called a solarium. This deck draws crowds of sightseers and sunbathers on pretty summer days. Now it is mostly vacant. Overhead heaters in the solarium radiate some warmth, but sleeping here in winter requires a good sleeping bag and plenty of warm clothes.

It is a gray, snowy afternoon as the *LeConte* departs. Small, dark-green islands pass and beyond them, tree-covered foothills that climb into mountainsides, and beyond them, white peaks of the Juneau Icefield. The Juneau and Stikine icefields of the Coast Mountains spawn many of the glaciers in Southeast. Glaciers in the northern tip of the region, in Glacier Bay and around Yakutat, come out of the Saint Elias Mountains, and its southern extension, the Fairweather Range. The Inside Passage is ice free except for stray bergs that pop up occasionally in a few stretches — in Icy Strait on the way to Pelican, or in Stephens Passage near the mouth of Tracy Arm, for instance. All the ferries are named after Alaska glaciers. The *LeConte* is namesake of LeConte Glacier at the head of LeConte Bay between Wrangell and Petersburg, the most southern tidewater glacier in North America.

As the ferry heads toward Hoonah, its engines throb. Big cast-iron pistons are pumping up and down in the engine room deep in the ship's bowels. Everything vibrates slightly. The seas are gentle, although the ship rocks side-to-side with changes in heading. Winds whip around the trailing edge of the solarium windows as the ship picks up speed entering Chatham Strait. The *LeConte* cruises at about 14 knots; the larger ships sail a few knots faster, about twice the speed of a fishing boat. A mist of icy water splatters the deck.

Three teenage boys don't seem to notice, and they bounce a hackey-sack to each other. The *LeConte* swarms with teenagers on this voyage. A boy's basketball team from the mostly Tlingit village of Angoon is traveling home from a game in Juneau. Nearly 50 kids are returning to Sitka after spending a week on a church-sponsored retreat at Douglas Island's Eaglecrest ski resort.

A thick veil of fog screens the base of the Chilkat Mountains from passengers aboard this Alaska state ferry cruising through Lynn Canal. The ferries call at two ports along the canal, Haines and Skagway, both of which are connected by roads to the continental highway system. (Mark Wayne)

Some of the most frequent riders of the ferries are Southeast's high school students. Basketball, baseball, track, soccer and wrestling teams routinely ride them to games, matches and tournaments. Some weeks during the school year they spend as much time on the ferries as in their regular classrooms. They bring their books and meet for study halls with their coaches. They all have stories about rough trips, when dinner plates slide off the tables and rope handles in the bathrooms finally have a purpose.

Southeast's Inside Passage is renown among mariners for its protected channels.

Sout...

The Saint Elias Mountains form the highest coastal range in the world, topped by Mount Saint Elias (18,008 feet) and Mount Vancouver (15,700 feet).

Malaspina Glacier is one of the largest ice masses on the North American continent — larger than the state of Rhode Island.

In 1990, an estimated 69,000 people lived in Southeastern Alaska — about three-fourths of them in five major urban areas: Juneau Ketchikan, Petersburg, Sitka and Wrangell.

The annual Southeast Alaska State Fair is held each August at Haines, drawing participants and spectators from all over Southeastern.

John Muir and a companion, missionary Samuel Hall Young, canoed through the Alexander Archipelago in 1879. Muir, naturalist, travel writer and later founder of the Sierra Club, was the first to systematically explore Glacier Bay and Muir Glacier.

United States-Canada Border

Haines Highway
to the Alaska Highway

Riggs Glacier
Muir Inlet
Muir Glacier
Carroll Glacier
Mount Harris 6,392

Grand Pacific Glacier

Tarr Inlet

Glacier Bay

Glacier Bay National Park & Preserve

Brady Icefield

Dundas Bay

Taylor Bay

Cape Spencer
Cross Sound

Icy Strait

Gustavus

Lemesurier Island

Elfin Cove
Port Althorp

Pelican

Lisianski Inlet

Yakobi Island

Chichagof Island

Frederick Ga...

Tenake...

Fairweather Range

Mount Fairweather 15,300'

Lituya Bay

Cape Fairweather

Mount Aylesworth 9,310'
Mount Armour 8,770'
Mount Duff 7,170'
Mount Wade 7,960'
Mount Herbert 6,090

Mount Jette 8,460'

Nunatak Fiord

Saint Elias Mountains

Alsek River

Harlequin Lake

Dry Bay

Mount Hubbard 15,015'

Mount Vancouver 15,700'

Hubbard Glacier

Russell Fiord

Saint

Yakutat Bay

Yakutat

Ocean Cape

Mount Augusta 14,070'

Mount Saint Elias 18,008'

Disenchantment Bay

Point Manby

Tyndall Glacier

Guyot Glacier

Icy Bay

Malaspina Glacier

United States-Canada Border

...heast Alaska

The world's greatest concentration of bald eagles is seen each fall and early winter along the Chilkat River, near Haines . . . up to 3,500 eagles in one small area.

Klondike Highway 2
to the Alaska Highway

White Pass and Yukon Railway
to Whitehorse

Chilkoot Pass

White Pass

Chilkat Inlet

Chilkoot Inlet

Skagway

Haines

Lynn Canal

Berners Bay

Mansfield Peninsula

Stephens Passage

Greens Creek Mine

Douglas Island

Douglas

Juneau

Mount Juneau ▲3,576'

Thane

Taku Taku River

Inlet

Juneau Icefield

Mount Bressler ▲7,856'

Mount Nesselrode ▲8,105'

Mount Ogilvie ▲7,700'

Mount London ▲7,550'

Mount Service ▲7,847'

Mount Poletica ▲7,620'

Mount Hitsop ▲7,164'

Mount Canning ▲6,967'

Mount Pullen ▲6,816'

▲Mount Bagot 7,150'

▲Snow Top 6,576'

Devils Paw ▲8,584'

Mount Ogden ▲7,484'

Mount Fremont Morse ▲6,734'

Mount Brundage ▲6,464'

Point Retreat

Port Snettisham

Stephens Passage

Glass Passage

Hoonah

Excursion

Greens Creek

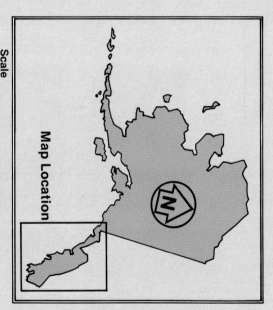

Map Location

Scale

Roads

Ferry Routes

50 kilometers

50 miles

Highways from the "outside world" reach tidewater at only three places in Southeastern — at Hyder, near Stewart, British Columbia; at Haines, where the Haines Highway begins its northward run to a meeting with the Alaska Highway; and at Skagway, where Klondike Highway 2 connects with the Alaska Highway near Whitehorse, Yukon Territory. The only other overland connection from tidewater is the White Pass and Yukon Railway from Skagway to Whitehorse.

The territorial capital was moved from Sitka to Juneau in 1906.

More than 95% of the land in Southeastern Alaska is under federal jurisdiction, Tongass National Forest

But when storms roar, high winds and confused seas can turn even the most seasoned sailor green. The *LeConte's* sister ship *Aurora* rode out one such storm Thanksgiving Day, 1984. Ninty-five-knot winds and 20-foot seas launched the ferry as if it were a surfboard, with its bow out of the water and the flying wings of the bridge riding the waves. Landing at Hoonah was impossible, for fear of crashing into the dock. Before it ended, the storm did $3 million damage to the boat harbor in Juneau and washed away four houses — practically the entire town — in Tenakee Springs. Roofs off houses and pieces of furniture floated in Clarence Strait for days afterward. Sometimes in bad weather, the ferries take refuge in protected coves or on the lee side of an island, but not that trip. "We were thankful to finally dock in Auke Bay (Juneau)," recalls seaman Lloyd Brooks.

■ ■ ■

Just as visitors to Southeast are charmed by the leisurely pace of ferry travel, residents of Southeast praise the utilitarian nature of the service. The ferries provide public transportation for locals. Some people commute to work on them. Since the ferries meet the highway network at five ports — Skagway, Haines, Hyder in summer only, Prince Rupert and Bellingham — they enable otherwise isolated coastal residents to drive to destinations outside.

The marine highway system is becoming increasingly important to tourism in the state. In 1992, the system carried 415,900 passengers — 7,200 more than the year before — and 111,600 vehicles. About 60,000 of these passengers were from outside the state.

Many of them began their ride in Bellingham or Prince Rupert, with some getting off at Ketchikan for a short stay, then reboarding the next north-bound ferry for other destinations. They may travel to Sitka and on to Juneau, where they end their trip with a flight home. Those traveling with a vehicle may continue on to Haines or Skagway and meet the road system. The ferries appeal to tourists who want more flexible schedules than those offered by many package tours. Reservations are issued on a first-come basis starting in December and summer bookings fill quickly.

"Tourists are always eager to go, always asking questions. You announce a pack of killer whales and the tourists pretty near roll the boat over running to the side to look," remarks Steve Hales, second mate on the *Aurora*. "The regulars, they see them over and over. They don't get excited."

The *Aurora* is one of the smaller ferries that makes shorter runs between outlying communities and larger towns. The crew and the regular passengers get to know each other by name. Most communities are at least three

The ferries call at Skagway, where passengers can try their hand at gold panning during the Tent City festival. (Harry M. Walker)

The state ferry system sometimes carries artists, storytellers or other entertainers who share their skills with passengers in exchange for reduced or free passage. Here Mickey Sonneborn, a watercolorist from Juneau, teaches Jeff Moreno, 10, how to use watercolor to capture his image of Southeast. Jeff's mother, Carol, looks on as the trio sits in the dining room of the ferry Malaspina. (L.J. Campbell, staff)

hours apart by ferry, so there is plenty of time on board for visiting, reading and sleeping. Riding a ferry, particularly the smaller vessels in winter when most of the passengers are locals, can be like spending time with extended family.

One of the *Aurora*'s weekly runs is between Ketchikan and Hollis on Prince of Wales Island. Each week, the ferry delivers about 28 vans of freight for communities connected to Hollis by road. It picks up children and takes them to orthodontic appointments in Ketchikan. It takes pregnant women to the hospital in Ketchikan and returns with moms and tiny newborns. A normal outing from the town of Craig is driving to Hollis to catch the ferry to Ketchikan for a day of shopping,

then returning on the ferry that night. Some people on the island are trying to get the Hollis terminal expanded, so larger ferries can dock as well.

"It's our highway and to have it cut off would be catastrophic," says Barbara Permenter, a Craig businesswoman. "We're always trying to educate the legislators and people in southwest and southcentral Alaska who don't realize what the ferry system is."

Many Southeasterners defend the marine highway almost automatically in casual conversation — the product of years of battling with people outside the region who see it as waste of state and federal money. The state spent about $31 million in 1992 to operate the marine highway, an 11 percent

reduction from the year before. The marine highway gets federal highway money for capital investments, in the same manner that the state gets federal money for its overland roads. Since no shipyard in Alaska can service the ferries, most of that money gets spent in the Lower 48, a fact that rankles some Alaska construction companies that bid on federally funded road work.

According to a 1992 study, the marine highway puts about $146 million back into the state's economy, in payroll, fuel and supply purchases, tourist dollars and other spending.

By providing relatively inexpensive transportation to regional shopping and business centers, the ferry system helps keep the cost of living in rural Southeast to levels below those of other rural areas of the state. The cost of living in Southeast is only about 10 percent higher than that of Anchorage, while the cost of living in interior Alaska is typically 30 to 40 percent above Anchorage. The system also helps keep money in the state that otherwise might go outside in catalog orders or buying trips.

The study also reported the system's impact on tourism and employment. Visitors to Alaska traveling the ferries spend about $46 million. In addition, some 800 of the system's 1,062 employees live in Southeast, earning

$30 million in payroll annually in jobs on ships and shore. If compared to the region's largest private employers, the Alaska Marine Highway System would rank near the top along with Ketchikan Pulp Co. Three-quarters of the system's Southeast employees live in Juneau and Ketchikan.

Phil Taylor, second mate on the *Malaspina*, is one of them. He grew up in Ketchikan, where kids are as likely to have skiffs as bicycles. He remembers as a child playing with a plastic model of the *Malaspina* until it wore out. Several years ago, a number of the models were discovered in a warehouse in Seattle where they had been stashed and forgotten many years earlier. The models, in their original boxes, are now for sale in the gift shops on board some of the ferries. Taylor never imagined working on the ships that he spent so much time riding as a youth. But today he can hardly imagine not living in Southeast. "I remember my first trip to the Interior," he recalls. "I wondered where all the trees were."

■ ■ ■

In 1993, the Alaska Marine Highway celebrates its 30th birthday. But the idea behind it is even older.

In Southeast, the most developed and settled region of Alaska until World War II, the idea of a government-operated ferry system was a perennial subject of public discussion during the early part of this century.

Ferries are not the only vessels plying Southeast waters. Pleasure craft, fishing boats and cruise ships of all sizes negotiate the watery passages. This cruise ship is anchored in Sitka Sound. (John Hyde)

During territorial days, passengers and freight traveled to Alaska mostly by Canadian cruise ships operating between Vancouver, British Columbia, and Skagway. Or they were carried out of Seattle by a motley fleet of American vessels salvaged from other uses. The primary air link was provided by Pan American Airways between Seattle, Ketchikan and Juneau. Not until 1937 did the first once-a-week air mail service begin from Juneau to Whitehorse, Yukon Territory, and on to Fairbanks.

The first comprehensive study of a coastal marine highway for Southeast came in 1944 from the North Pacific Commission. It suggested linking coastal communities by ferry, to extend the broader Alaska and continental highway system, and to promote tourism by tapping into the motoring public of North America. But the report concluded that a privately operated system could not support itself year-round.

World War II changed transportation in Alaska considerably. It brought a road system and spurred development of aviation in the territory. Post-war Alaska grew in population. Tourism picked up. Those two factors and the discontinuation of marine-based carriers from Seattle renewed interest in a marine highway for Southeast. A regular highway would have taken miles of bridges. The marine highway was a unique alternative to extending roads to this large, sparsely populated region of formidable topography.

The first step in the Southeast ferry system was taken in 1949 when Haines businessmen Steve Homer and Ray Gelotte launched service between Haines, Skagway and Tee Harbor near Juneau. They converted a war surplus Navy landing craft into the ferry *Chilkoot* that could carry 13 vehicles and 20 passengers. Although the *Chilkoot* stayed busy, it was too small to be profitable. By 1951, the service was in the hands of the Territorial

Board of Road Commissioners. In 1957, the *Chilkoot* was retired and replaced with the larger *Chilkat*.

Four studies from 1949 through 1959 recommended expanding the ferry system. In 1960, voters approved an $18 million bond issue for three ships and seven docks in Southeast with service to Prince Rupert, and for one ship and docks in the Southwest Alaska area. The new system started in 1963.

During its first full year of operation, the system carried 84,000 people and 16,000 vehicles, far more than planners had anticipated. In 1964, the *Tustumena* began serving Southwest Alaska. In 1967, service was extended to Seattle, and the next year the *Wickersham* was added to the fleet. During the following decade, the system continued

developing, adding several new vessels, including the *Aurora*, the *LeConte* and the *Columbia* to replace the *Wickersham*. In 1989, Bellingham replaced Seattle as the southernmost port. In 1992 design work began on a new vessel, the first since the *Aurora* came on line in 1977. The new ship is expected in service by summer 1996, to replace the *Malaspina*.

■ ■ ■

The *Malaspina* heads out from Sitka en route to Ketchikan. The snow-covered crater of Mount Edgecumbe, an extinct volcano on Kruzof Island to the west, looms on the horizon of Sitka Sound. The route north from Sitka cuts between small islands, across a stretch of open ocean, through a series of tricky narrows between Baranof and Chichagof islands, and into Peril Strait. During Russian occupation in the 1800s, a party of Native sea otter hunters died here after eating poisoned mussels. For years there has been talk of shortening the route with a ferry dock on the northeast side of Baranof Island in Rodman Bay, closer to Chatham Strait, and connecting the terminal to Sitka with a road across the island.

The way it runs now, the ferry navigates close to shore through a sampling of the scenery for which Southeast is famous — rocky shores, rain forests, quiet coves, layers of blues, greens, grays and pinks. An hour or

Capt. Ervin L. Hagerup, master of the Malaspina, *looks up from morning duty in the pilot house. At the wheel is Dave Strangio, able seaman. Thomas R. Reed, chief mate, enters the pilot house off the flying bridge. (L.J. Campbell, staff)*

FACING PAGE: *Granite spires cradle pockets of ice in the Juneau Icefield in the Coast Mountains behind Juneau, the region's largest city. The mountains are visible to ferry passengers along much of the Inside Passage route. (John Hyde)*

staff and a small cadre of officers. The *Malaspina* is one of the system's larger ships at 408 feet, with room for 500 passengers and 107 vehicles. This trip takes the ship and her crew from Juneau to Sitka, Petersburg, Wrangell, Ketchikan, Prince Rupert and Bellingham. Then they reverse the route going north.

"The ship is like a family," says Capt. Ervin Hagerup, master of the *Malaspina*. Hagerup came up through the "hawse pipe," mariner's lingo for working up through the ranks. His career started in 1966, although at the time it was just a good summer job, washing pots and pans on the *Taku*. A few summers later, he got his first break as a waiter in the officer's mess where he met the men who would teach him to steer. He finally nabbed an opening on the deck crew. Working on the ships interested him more than his college architectural courses, so he hired on full time. Soon he was studying for his pilot's license. The day he passed, "I kissed that license. I said that's all I'll ever need."

His euphoria was short-lived. Two new ships were coming on line and opportunities to advance came quickly, from third mate to second mate to chief mate. The third and second mates do piloting; the chief mate deals with personnel, time sheets, payroll. He started studying for his master's license and soon moved into a relief master position, filling in as captain where needed. In 1986, Hagerup became a master of the *Malaspina*. But 27 years working on the ferries took a toll on his marriage, which ended in divorce

so out of Sitka, a voice comes over the ship's loudspeaker. Passengers perk up. Often the captain or a mate in the pilot's house will announce sightings of wildlife — porpoises, whales, eagles, bears — or interesting landmarks. The voice continues: A flock of pink flamingos are overwintering on Highwater Island, apparently blown off their migratory course, according to ship biologist, Dr. Robin Cormorant.

A couple of long-liners from Sitka, who have been talking on the upper deck about fishing, look at each other.

The voice returns: Sharp-eyed observers can see the flamingos roosting about 50 feet above the beach in the trees. A man in short sleeves and down vest runs frantically along the rail with his camera, alternately saying,

"Where are they? I can't see them," and "This can't be real." The ship passes. Six bright pink birds sit perfectly still on dark green boughs — like the carefully placed ornaments they are. The Sitka fishermen grin.

Up in the pilothouse, the *Malaspina*'s officers wonder how the joke went over with the passengers. No one knows for sure where the flamingos came from. Someone says bored loggers flew the plastic birds to their roost in a helicopter. Another attributes the prank to a couple of crew members who have a hunting cabin nearby.

It breaks up the trip a bit. Crew members work one- and two-week shifts. The hours are long and the work demanding. The *Malaspina*'s 50-member crew is made up of the steward's staff, the deck crew, engineering

when he refused to leave the sea.

It is late in the night when the ship enters Wrangell Narrows, a treacherous passage between Petersburg and Wrangell. Buoys with flashing red and green lights mark the channel, which is so tight in places that the lights seem to pass within arm's length of the ship. Because of the way the lights look at night, the narrows are sometimes called "Christmas Tree Lane" or "Pinball Alley." Able seaman Doran Groves stands watch at the point of the bow, a bitterly cold duty in the night wind. Behind him in the warmth of the forward observation lounge, an Elderhostel group of older tourists from the Lower 48 watch the light show. Some of them have bundled up to ride through the narrows on the outside deck, but, unlike Groves at his exposed post, they periodically duck into doorways to escape the wind.

The narrows are winding and shallow with tricky currents, and navigators have little room for error. Once committed, a ship has to continue through. If conditions are known to be bad, the ships just don't go.

Ferries skirt the northern edge of Chichagof Island as they pass by Port Althorp. Capt. George Vancouver anchored here in 1794, when he named the waterway for the eldest son of Earl Spencer, who that year became First Lord of the British Admiralty. (Bruce H. Baker)

LEFT: *More sleek and maneuverable than the Alaska Marine Highway ferries are the sailboats that find safe anchorages tucked away in a Southeast cove. Here the* Mistral of Sitka *rides the calm waters of Fords Terror southeast of Juneau. (R.E. Johnson)*

ABOVE: *Young entrepreneurs at Mount Edgecumbe High School in Sitka market their own product, smoked salmon. (Ernest Manewal)*

Even at times when everything seems to be fine, the narrows can throw some nasty surprises, like instant fog in an place aptly called Blind Slough. Hagerup recalls the time a ship slammed into a buoy and ripped an 11-foot gash in the bow while trying to avoid a fishing boat in this stretch. "The narrows just take a little extra attention," he says now, standing watch in the corner of the pilot house, scanning the water ahead with binoculars.

The second mate is navigating. He stands behind the front windows of the bridge. He watches for navigational beacons on the

horizon that signal course changes. He monitors a dizzying array of electronic instruments at his side, including radar screens that translate the sea floor, coast line and objects in the water into a video display of colored pixels. He calls out course headings rapidly "...20 east to 10, east to 20, east to 5, 171..." that are repeated and executed by the seaman behind him at the wheel. He knows the course by memory; a license requirement for pilots in Southeast is memorizing several dozen navigational charts and describing water depths, land formations and sailing conditions in every season.

This trip through the narrows goes smoothly. The crew relaxes when the last flashing buoy passes. "That was a nice slide show," says Hagerup, "Just slide on through."

■ ■ ■

The state ferries touch every Southeast community. They are floating vats of regional cultures, attitudes and issues peppered by outside values. As the ports come and go, people do too. Passengers often have time to get off for a walk, sightseeing, shopping. At Tenakee Springs, there might even be time for a soak in the sulfur springs located inside the bath house at the head of the dock. Back on board, the scene continues.

Mickey Sonneborn, a watercolor artist from Juneau, paints at a table on the *Malaspina*.

She is heading south on vacation and is traveling the ferry as part of its "arts and education on board" program.

Several years ago, the system started bringing aboard artists, musicians, storytellers and performers to entertain guests. Often wildlife biologists from the Alaska Department of Fish and Game or from the U.S. Forest Service travel on the ferries to talk about marine mammals, birds, plants and other natural sights. Most of this happens during the summer tourist season, but even now in the middle of winter, Sonneborn is earning her passage.

A couple of young boys sit across from her, asking all sorts of questions about how to

paint what they've been seeing. The youngest boy, Jeff Moreno, 10, is particularly curious and Mickey sets him up with paper and a brush. His brother, Scott, 13, watches. Mickey coaches Jeff and soon he holds up his finished picture, a seascape with rocks and trees. He stands up with the picture as his dad starts a video camera. "This is a painting I did with Mickey," he says to the camera. "It's of Southeast Alaska...and I did it on the *Malaspina*."

The family is leaving Alaska, moving from Juneau to Albany, N. Y., where their dad has a new job. "We thought going out on the ferry would be real special," says their mom, Carol. "This is real special."

The red-roofed Pioneer's Home and St. Michael's Cathedral mark the heart of downtown Sitka, population 8,588. Roads run north around the base of Harbor Mountain to the ferry terminal and Starrigavan Campground, and south along Sawmill Creek Blvd. to just beyond the pulp mill at Silver Bay. (Rex Melton)

Southeast Alaska:
A Closer Look

■ Ketchikan ■

Ketchikan, the fourth largest city in Alaska, is a hard-working fishing and timber town — the manufacturing center of Southeast. It is picturesque with its bustling waterfront and cliff-hanging houses, and politically conservative with a fringe of green.

Thousands of people visit here each year. They see totem poles. They watch performances of flamboyant Tlingit dancers. They catch halibut and king salmon, hunt mountain goat and deer, adventure into the wilds of Misty Fiords National Monument. They shop and hike, visit museums, see salmon at Deer Mountain hatchery, and tour the city's biggest employer, Ketchikan Pulp mill. And they probably get wet; Ketchikan averages 13 feet of rain each year.

Located on Revillagigedo Island, Ketchikan is the first Alaska port for ships traveling north. In 1992, about 257,000 visitors came to Ketchikan on cruises. Revillagigedo, locally called Revilla, is cut from the mainland by Behm Canal. The canal's traffic includes nuclear submarines headed to a Navy noise testing facility on Back Island, north of Ketchikan.

Ketchikan snakes along Revilla's southwest shore, facing the waters of Tongass Narrows. Nearly 14,000 people live in Ketchikan Gateway Borough, which includes Gravina Island across the narrows. The city airport is

on Gravina, served by ferry from Ketchikan. There has long been talk of bridging the narrows, to improve airport access and open up land for the town's expansion; the link would cost $60 million to $130 million.

Everything comes to Ketchikan through the narrows. Floatplanes, cargo barges, fishing boats, cruise ships, state ferries and log ships work the waterfront constantly. Ketchikan is the transportation, medical, banking and retail center for the region, including towns and logging camps on nearby islands. Fishing boats sell their catch and replenish supplies here. The town's numerous bars turn rowdy when crews hit shore.

Ketchikan's business district stretches along the narrows on tall pilings above 23-foot tide extremes. Frame homes find a purchase on

FACING PAGE: *Once notorious as the home of the ladies of the line, Ketchikan's Creek Street is now one of the preferred locations for the town's craft and tourist shops. (John Warden)*

the cliffs above, reached by steep wooden staircases and plank streets. Land is so tight that the city has the highest population density of any Alaska town — 2,754 people per square mile.

The town's only highway runs between the water and cliffs along a narrow shelf of shore and over concrete viaducts. It goes 18 miles north — past McDonald's, the new indoor mall, the ferry dock, the post office, the pulp mill — to Settler's Cove campground. It goes 16 miles south through the Native community

With the highest population density of any Alaska town, 2,754 people per square mile, Ketchikan clings to a narrow shelf between Tongass Narrows and the steep-sloped peaks of Revillagigedo Island. A ferry connects Ketchikan with its airport on Gravina Island. (Mary Ida Henrikson)

PERFECT PARTNERS
ALASKAN GOLD | AUSTRALIAN OPAL

OPAL SHOWROOM   GEM CUTTER

LEFT: *A Swedish-made funicular links pedestrians on Creek Street with Cape Fox Lodge more than 100 feet above. (Harry M. Walker)*

ABOVE: *Andi Smith opened The 5-Star Cafe in 1991, in a renovated dance hall and brothel on Creek Street. (L.J. Campbell, staff)*

of Saxman. It is one of the busiest two-lanes in Alaska with 20,000 cars a day; a $70-million upgrade is slated for the late 1990s.

Downtown — with its curio shops, historic hotels, art galleries, restaurants and offices — occupies a delta near the mouth of Ketchikan Creek. White settlers started a fish saltery here in the 1880s. Pink salmon ran thick; this had long been the site of a summer fish camp for Tlingit Indians, who called it Kitschk-him or Ketschk's stream.

Mining, not fishing, brought the first crowds to Ketchikan. Gold and copper on nearby islands made Ketchikan a rendezvous point for miners, lawyers and others, including prostitutes who opened brothels all over town. Soon after the town's incorporation in 1900, city fathers moved the ladies to Creek Street, a plank boardwalk edging the banks of Ketchikan Creek; it was considered a more discreet place for "sporting women" to carry on, according to *Spirit! Historic Ketchikan, Alaska* (1992). Today the restored historic "homes" of Creek Street are open as eateries, galleries, book stores and espresso bars. A glassed-in tram carries people from Creek Street up to a new hotel overlooking the city.

The collapsed copper market in 1907 choked mining. But Ketchikan was becoming the "salmon capital of the world." The fishery grew rapidly from one successful cannery and saltery in 1890. A big sawmill produced lumber for buildings and fish packing boxes. By 1930, the town had 13 canneries and freezers, a fleet of nearly 1,000 salmon boats and a substantial halibut fishery. The halibut fishermen, mostly Norwegians, made up a large community.

The U.S. Lighthouse Service came to help with navigation, search and rescue. Its base became the Coast Guard's, which expanded during World War II to more than 750 personnel. Today, the Coast Guard in

Ketchikan employs 200 people and polices the entire region.

In the 1950s, the town's economy shifted from declining fisheries to timber. Ketchikan Pulp Co. opened its mill at Ward Cove in 1954, part of a federal effort to encourage industry in Southeast. The mill is now owned by Louisiana Pacific Corp. and employs about 550. Logging in the Ketchikan district of Tongass National Forest employs as many or more some years. The industry has widespread support in Ketchikan, including that of the local newspaper. Critics are generally considered to be naive and misinformed, although an outspoken faction against logging persists. Those who take even a moderate stance risk being labeled tree-huggers.

Living with copious amounts of rain may be the biggest daily challenge. People are used to playing and working in the wet. For a break, music, theater, ballet, ethnic dance and art shows are among events sponsored in part by the Ketchikan Area Arts and Humanities Council. The city's Totem Heritage Center, with the state's largest collection of original totem poles, offers an ambitious schedule of classes in Native art and culture.

Fishing continues as an important way of life. Some 300 people hold commercial fishing licenses and in summer, nearly 1,000 people work at the town's three fish processors. Tourism is expected to only get bigger. The city is looking at a new dock to handle 800-foot ships, expansion of the Ketchikan Shipyard is planned, and so is a new convention center. Development of a ski resort and an aquarium is being considered. Downtown at the site of the original sawmill, the U.S. Forest Service is building a $7 million interpretive center, the Southeast Alaska Public Lands Information Center, to help the region's thousands of visitors understand what they are seeing.

Southeast Wildlands

National Parks, Preserves, Monuments, Wilderness and National Wildlife Refuges

Land Use Designation (LUD) II Management Areas*

*Land Use Designation (LUD) II Management Areas are lands managed by the U. S. Department of Agriculture, Forest Service. In 1990 for the first time in any national forest, Congress set aside in Tongass a dozen LUD II areas off-limits to logging, generally roadless and managed to retain their wildland character.

1 - Wrangell-Saint Elias National Park & Preserve
2 - Russell Fiord Wilderness
3 - Glacier Bay National Park & Preserve
4 - Chilkat Bald Eagle Preserve (state-owned)
5 - Pleasant/Lemesurier/Inian Islands Wilderness
6 - Endicott River Wilderness
7 - West Chichagof-Yakobi Wilderness
8 - Young Lake Wilderness
9 - Admiralty Island National Monument Kootznoowoo Wilderness
10 - Tracy Arm-Fords Terror Wilderness
11 - Chuck River Wilderness
12 - Saint Lazaria Island NWR
13 - South Baranof Wilderness
14 - Tebenkof Bay-Kuiu Wilderness
15 - Petersburg Creek-Duncan Salt Chuck Wilderness
16 - Stikine-LeConte Wilderness
17 - Hazy Islands NWR
18 - Coronation Island Wilderness
19 - Warren & Maurelle Islands Wilderness
20 - Karta River Wilderness
21 - South Etolin Wilderness
22 - Misty Fiords National Monument Wilderness
23 - South Prince of Wales Wilderness
24 - Wolf Rock NWR
25 - Lowrie, Forrester & Petrel Islands NWR
26 - Yakutat Forelands
27 - Berners Bay
28 - Anan Creek
29 - Kadashan
30 - Lisianski River/Upper Hoonah Sound
31 - Mount Calder/Mount Holbrook
32 - Nutkwa
33 - Outside Islands
34 - Trap Bay
35 - Point Adolphus/Mud Bay
36 - Naha
37 - Salmon Bay

(ALASKA GEOGRAPHIC® map by Kathy Doogan)

This map shows areas managed to maintain their wildland character. This represents about 45 percent of Southeast, and covers glaciated, alpine, wetland and forested areas within various federal and state conservation units. It also includes 6.5 million acres protected from commercial logging within 16.9-million-acre Tongass National Forest. Commercial timber grows on only part of this acreage. See the pull-out map included with this book for Tongass in its entirety.

■ Saxman ■

The Tlingit village of Saxman is located 2.5 miles south of Ketchikan. Its 370 people accommodate more than 20,000 visitors each summer who come to see their totem poles, Native dancers and artists.

Saxman dates to the 1890s, settled primarily as a school site. The people of Cape Fox village, on the mainland off Revillagigedo Channel, and of Tongass village, on nearby Tongass Island in Nakat Bay, were told they could have one school. So in 1894, they merged villages at a new location on Revillagigedo Island. They named their new village after Presbyterian minister Samuel Saxman, who had drowned in the first expedition to find a site.

A Presbyterian mission school opened in 1895. Within two years, the village had 120 people, a store and sawmill. A road to Ketchikan was built in 1925.

In 1938, the U.S. Forest Service began retrieving totem poles from abandoned villages and cemeteries on Tongass, Cat, Village and Pennock islands and from Cape Fox. Reproductions were carved of the most deteriorated poles. In Saxman, originals and reproductions were erected in Totem Park.

Today at the park, a Tlingit tribal house, the largest in Southeast, hosts the Cape Fox Dancers in summer. In winter, socials known as the Monthly Grind draw several hundred people, mostly from Ketchikan. Winter entertainment revolves around basketball. The Natives of Saxman belong to Cape Fox village corporation, which owns 23,040 acres of mostly timber. Cape Fox's 72-room lodge, a grand affair styled like a Tlingit tribal house with exposed spruce beams, carvings and totem poles, opened 1990 in Ketchikan above Creek Street. Cape Fox Tours, another village corporation enterprise, offers guided visits through the tribal house, totem park and totem carving shed.

The city and village corporation provide local jobs, and some people work in Ketchikan. Saxman once had a local fishing fleet of about a dozen boats, but now most of the town's fishermen hire out as crew members.

City manager Joe Williams, a Saxman-born Tlingit who lived in Anchorage 18 years, returned to the village to raise his six children. "Small town raising kids is really where it's at," he says.

Some members of the Cape Fox Dancers perform during the summer months as visitors arrive at the Beaver tribal house at Saxman. Tribal symbols adorn the houseposts and screen at rear. The beaver's tail appears below representations of the beaver's four front teeth decorated with eyes and faces; the more eyes and faces, the more powerful is the symbol. The dancers are from left: front row, Kelly White, Richard Shields Jr., Chris Phillips; rear: Forest DeWitt Jr., the late Albert Shields Jr., Sara Abbott, Cheryl DeWitt and Kevin Shields. (John Warden)

■ Hyder ■

Portland Canal, a 70-mile-long saltwater fiord, forms the southern boundary between Alaska and British Columbia. At its head nestles the once-booming mining town of Hyder. About 100 people live here.

Hyder joins the larger town of Stewart, British Columbia, by a 2.5-mile gravel road cut along steep granite cliffs. The road leads from Stewart to the Cassiar Highway, about 40 miles away.

In the late 1890s, prospectors found gold and silver in nearby hills. When Canadian prospects proved workable in 1901, Stewart sprang into being. On the American side, the village of Portland Canal struggled on the homestead of the Lindeborg brothers. In 1915, prospectors were denied their request for a post office; postal authorities said too many Portlands already existed. They then chose the name Hyder, for Canadian mining engineer Frederick B. Hyder, who had predicted a great future for the area.

In 1917, rich silver deposits discovered in Canada's upper Salmon River basin turned Hyder into the ocean port, supply point and post office for the district. The Reverdy Mountains behind camp meant Hyder grew on pilings over the tide flats. During the 1920s the town boomed with probably 500 people living in the area.

Gold, silver, copper, lead and zinc mining, mostly from the Riverside Mine, occurred from 1924 through 1950. Tungsten was mined during World War II. The Granduc copper mine in Canada moved ore to Stewart, until the mine closed in 1984.

Today, summer tourists visit Hyder, by road from Canada or on weekly state ferry runs from Ketchikan. The state operates a small boat ramp, and mail is delivered by floatplane. The town has a few cafes, bars and inns, while Stewart offers more services including public schools attended by the children of Hyder. Sightseeing attractions include the oldest masonry building in Alaska, a storehouse constructed in 1896; tours of Salmon Glacier; and a viewing platform to see large chum salmon runs and feeding black bears.

From the water, Hyder, population about 100, looks just like what it is, a sleepy outpost at the head of Portland Canal. Two miles away lies larger Stewart, British Columbia. The two towns are connected to the continental highway system by a 40-mile spur to the Cassiar Highway. Hyder has drier summers than many other Southeast communities, but its winters usually bring heavy snow. (Charlie Crangle)

Mysterious Misty Fiords

Misty Fiords National Monument — an aptly named region of steep-walled fiords and frequent rain — covers 2,294,343 million acres at the southern end of Southeast. It extends from Portland Canal north across the Unuk River, east to the Canadian border and west to include a slice of Revillagigedo Island.

The monument encompasses dramatic wilderness — unspoiled coastal habitats of fiords, sea cliffs, glaciers, waterfalls, granite mountain peaks, and old-growth rain forests. In the monument's wet climate, bare rock is quickly colonized by mosses, small plants, shrubs and trees, which cling in places to near vertical slopes. Practically the entire spectrum of Southeast's wildlife occurs here.

Extensive glaciation gouged the fiords and sculpted valleys and basins some 10,000 years ago, and glaciers today feed the monument's rivers. Past volcanic activity shows up, too. A volcanic plug forms New Eddystone Rock, a prominent landmark popular with seals in east Behm Canal at the mouth of Rudyerd Bay. Less than 120 years ago, a basalt flow partially dammed Blue River, in the northeastern part of the monument.

A molybdenum deposit at Quartz Hill inside the monument is thought to be the world's largest. In 1980, the Alaska National Interest Lands Conservation Act designated all the monument as wilderness except 156,210 acres to accommodate the deposit's potential development.

The best way to visit Misty Fiords is by boat or plane. Several companies out of Ketchikan offer tours by yacht and floatplane. Ketchikan is the closest city, 50 miles away by water and 20 minutes by air. Deep Behm Canal cuts through the monument, providing passage for a growing number of cruise ships. The tiny town of Hyder, only 18 miles by trail from the monument's eastern border, offers a little used overland approach.

National forest service rangers

patrol the monument by kayak in summer from a wilderness camp at the head of Rudyerd Bay. Among other duties, these "kayak rangers" board cruise ships and give talks. Tourism in Misty Fiords, like elsewhere in Southeast, is rapidly growing; an estimated 50,000 people visited the monument in 1992.

Some hardy kayakers paddle out from Ketchikan, although most get a lift to Rudyerd Bay or Walker Cove on the tour boats. Storms can blow up with little notice in Misty Fiords, with southeast winds churning large waves on Behm Canal.

The U.S. Forest Service maintains 14 cabins and four shelters within the monument. Finding a good camp site can be tricky; tides fluctuate 25 feet daily so beach meadows that look enticing may be flooded within hours. Several wilderness lodges operate nearby and within the monument.

LEFT: *Boats congregate off Kirk Point, in Misty Fiords National Monument, during a herring sac-roe fishery. The water is milky with herring milt from spawning males. (Chip Porter)*

FACING PAGE: *Water tumbles from a landslide caused by steep terrain and heavy rains in Misty Fiord National Monument's Rudyerd Bay, about 50 miles by boat from Ketchikan. Fractured, 3,000-foot granite cliffs line parts of Punchbowl Cove in the bay. These fractures formed deep within the earth before the area was uplifted millions of years ago. (Chip Porter)*

■ Myers Chuck ■

The quiet community of Myers Chuck, or Meyers Chuck, sits in a cove off Clarence Strait on the tip of the Cleveland Peninsula 40 miles northwest of Ketchikan. Here many a fishing vessel has ridden out a southeast storm that frothed the waters of Clarence Strait into mountainous swells.

Myers Chuck has about 40 people. They fish for salmon, crab, clams, rockfish and halibut. They trap and hunt, gather wood for heating, and keep their electrical generators going. The community has a lodge and post office, phones, mail by plane and satellite television. The school serves as a community center. Since the general store closed in the early 1990s, people boat across Clarence Strait to Thorne Bay on Prince of Wales Island, or fly or boat south to Ketchikan. Or they call in orders to be delivered by floatplane. They supplement their needs with income from jobs outside.

The history of the place depends on who does the telling. One story says an old sailboat captain, Verne Myers, arrived in 1881 with seven men and built a two-story log cabin. Another says the village was named for a prospector who found his food in the nearby woods. Records show a Mr. Myers fished a red salmon stream on nearby Union Bay in

---

FACING PAGE: *Commercial fishing dominates the economy of Metlakatla, a Tsimshian Indian community on Annette Island, about 15 miles by boat from Ketchikan. The twin-steeples of Duncan Memorial Church (the original burned in 1948) look out over the town of 1,600 founded by Father William Duncan and 400 of his followers in 1887. Metlakatla is the only federal Indian reservation in Alaska. (Don Pitcher)*

1898 and sold his fish to the Loring cannery.

In 1911, M.E. Lane started a small hand-pack cannery here. In 1914, his operation was classified as a mild-cure station where salmon were lightly salted before shipment. He soon after sold the saltery, the last mention of permanent fish processing in Myers Chuck.

The largest cannery in the area operated nearby in Union Bay from 1916 to 1945. Floating mild-cure stations came each spring to buy chinook salmon from the trollers, who found safe harbor at Myers Chuck. The early community included a store, dock and float with postal service starting in 1922. Cabins occupied land leased from the federal government until 1934, when the town site was withdrawn from Tongass National Forest.

■ Metlakatla ■

Neatly laid out on the west shore Port Chester on Annette Island is Metlakatla, a community of about 1,600.

Commercial fishing, two sawmills, a salmon cannery and cold storage make up the town's main economy. Visitors come occasionally — the state ferry provides service and locally owned Taquan Air has regular floatplane flights — but tourism has never taken hold.

"In the summer, everyone's too busy anyway," says lifelong resident Frieda Jackson, laughing.

Metlakatla, a mostly Tsimshian Indian community, is the first and only federal Indian reservation in Alaska. Its status allows use of fish traps, outlawed elsewhere in the state long ago.

Religious migration of Tsimshian Indians led to Metlakatla's founding. William Duncan, a Scottish lay preacher from the Church of England, led a group of Tsimshians

from Fort Simpson, British Columbia, to Old Metlakatla near Prince Rupert. The model community thrived for 20 years until Duncan quarreled with the church.

He then led a devoted group of 400 to Annette Island, to an unoccupied former Tlingit village. They patterned the new colony after Old Metlakatla, with generous homesites, gardens, cannery, sawmill, stores and a large church. They dedicated it on Aug. 7, 1887. Four years later, Congress declared Annette Island a reservation.

Today, this well-engineered community is largely self-contained with many amenities — clothing shops, restaurants, grocery, bank, three video stores, two gasoline stations, clinic with resident doctors and dentist, police station, volunteer fire department, senior center and apartment complex. The high school features an Olympic-size pool, weight room and sauna open to public use. Basketball consumes almost everyone in winter.

In summer, about 110 local boats fish commercially for salmon, halibut and herring. Divers harvested sea cucumbers commercially the first time in winter 1993. Subsistence fishing, hunting deer and gathering beach foods such as seaweed, clams, mussels, lady's slippers and gum boots continues year-round. When people need a break, they likely drive their boats 15 miles to Ketchikan.

Today, worshipers still attend the Duncan Memorial Church; numerous other denominations include Jehovah Witness, Salvation Army, Bible Baptist and Presbyterian. Duncan's cottage is restored as a museum.

The town is governed by the Metlakatla Indian Community, with a mayor and council. Permits are required for extended visits.

■ Prince of Wales ■

Prince of Wales Island in southern Southeast holds a sizable chunk of the region's forests, roads, minerals and people. Its economy hinges on catching fish, cutting down trees and enticing visitors.

At 2,231 square miles, Prince of Wales is Southeast's largest island and the nation's third largest, behind Hawaii and Kodiak. About 75 percent of the timber harvested in the Ketchikan area of Tongass National Forest comes from Prince of Wales. With this logging has come the most extensive road network in Southeast.

The island's mineral deposits — copper, gold, lead, zinc, uranium, marble, limestone — supported a flurry of mining during the early 1900s. Mineral companies prospecting Prince of Wales and its neighboring islands today consider the area to be a storehouse of riches waiting for a ripe market.

About 4,300 people live year-round on the island, according to the 1990 federal census. The number swells by several thousand during the peak of summer logging, commercial fishing and tourism.

Nearly half the island's permanent residents live in Craig and Klawock, while another quarter of them live in the next three largest towns of Thorne Bay, Hydaburg and Coffman Cove. The rest live in smaller communities and the half-dozen logging camps that come and go along the island's coast. Another couple of hundred people live in logging camps on nearby islands.

Tim Minicucci fishes the Karta River off Kasaan Bay on the east coast of Prince of Wales Island. (Chip Porter)

Nathan Brewer and Alistair Findlay inspect remains from Prince of Wales' mining tradition at the Copper Mountain mines. Deposits of copper, gold, lead, zinc, uranium, marble and limestone generated interest among miners in the early 1900s. Marble from nearby Marble Island, quarried from 1909 through 1932, can be seen in the pillars of the Capitol in Juneau. (Dee Randolph)

The five biggest towns are connected by about 300 miles of mainline road criss-crossing the northern half of the island. One stretch across the island is paved; the remaining roads are gravel. Several thousand miles of logging roads lace the island; many of these roads are blocked off as logging an area ends. Hunters use these abandoned roads in their chase of the island's deer and black bears.

Large-scale harvesting of Tongass National Forest timber on the island started in the 1950s when the Ketchikan Pulp Co. mill opened. In 1971, the Alaska Native Claims

Settlement Act allotted about 92,000 acres on the island to four Native village corporations.

Logging on Prince of Wales peaked in 1989 with about 500 million board feet; 240 million board feet of that was from private lands. Roughly 278 million board feet were cut in 1992, mostly of national forest timber.

Harvests of Native-owned old-growth is winding down.

The U.S. Forest Service classifies about 1.45 million acres of Tongass on Prince of Wales as forested, and manages 664,530 acres for timber production. Of that, 158,903 acres had been logged through 1992.

The majority of Craig's 1,800 residents turn to the sea to support the commerce of Prince of Wales Island's largest town. Salmon, shrimp, halibut, abalone, bottomfish, Dungeness crab, herring, herring roe, rockfish, clams, sea urchins and sea cucumbers contributed to a seafood economy with a 1989-to-1991 average value for all species of $3.85 million. (Don Pitcher)

A female red-breasted merganser and her chicks check for danger. This species usually nests on the ground rather than in hollow trees like other merganser species. Their long, serrated bill aids in catching their chief prey, fish. (Pat Costello)

Growth through the 1980s resulted in two former logging camps incorporating as towns. In 1992, phone service was extended to a half-dozen remote communities. A 4.5 megawatt hydroelectric facility at Black Bear Lake planned by Alaska Power and Telephone might come on line by the late 1990s. Several towns are expanding their docks to spur waterfront commerce. The Prince of Wales Chamber of Commerce formed along with an islandwide advisory committee that communicates islanders' needs to the state.

Maintaining ferry service ranks as a priority. The island is served regularly by floatplanes and cargo barge, and many people own boats. But the ferry connects Prince of Wales by highway, the only way to drive on and off the island since there is no bridge. "Our only chance of a hard link is continental drift," says Craig city planner Jon Bolling. The airport near Klawock is slated to get lights in 1993 and navigation equipment, perhaps by 1994, that will enable all-weather use by cargo and passenger jets.

Prince of Wales' growing popularity with sport fishermen translates into more charter operators, motels and upscale wilderness lodges. The island's road system meets the state ferry from Ketchikan at Hollis.

The U.S. Forest Service opened Eagle's Nest Campground, two miles east of Control Lake on the road system, in 1990 to accommodate the increasing number of recreational vehicles. In addition, the forest service has four other tent campgrounds and 20 cabins on the island.

An extensive cave network in limestone karsts on the island's north end — with the nation's first and third deepest caves — continues to be explored and charted, eliciting excitement among caving enthusiasts throughout the nation. The forest service in 1993 was developing visitor access to at least one cavern; a viewing platform overlooks another cave entrance where salmon spawn.

CRAIG

This once-seasonal Indian fish camp has grown into the largest town on Prince of Wales. Located in the middle of the island's west coast off San Alberto Bay, Craig is near the rich fishing grounds of the outer islands and open ocean. It is also the goods and services capital of the island with a large grocery, gas station and garage, bank, clothing, hardware and gift stores, one doctor, three dentists, and — new in 1993 — an espresso bar.

About 1,800 people live in Craig, according to the city. The population has tripled since 1980, largely because of increased logging on Native lands.

Salmon historically and currently is the

main fishery. Shrimp, halibut, abalone, bottomfish, crab, herring, herring roe and sea cucumbers also are harvested; as one local said, "If it's in the water, we take it out." About 250 Craig residents hold commercial fishing licenses. During summer, the town swarms with hundreds more fishermen in salmon seiners. Two fish buyers operate cold storages, sending the catch to Ketchikan for processing.

In 1992, the city obtained 600 acres of tideland from the state and plans numerous waterfront developments, including a deep-water harbor, marine industrial park and 60 more boat slips. A new water treatment plant provides clean water for ice production and future fish processing. A privately owned 50-ton boat lift allows maintenance and long-term dry storage of boats.

Originally, Natives came to nearby Fish Egg Island to gather herring roe in spring. In 1907, Craig Millar packed boxes of lightly salted salmon on Fish Egg Island for a German fish company. The next year, he opened a permanent station on a larger nearby island. In 1911, Lindenberger Packing Co. expanded Millar's operation with a freezer and then a cannery, at the time the second-largest in Alaska. The settlement became known as Craig.

Meanwhile Millar built a cannery to the southwest. Today, the buildings house Waterfall Cannery Resort. Ethel Carle Yates, 74, remembers when she and her family used to come to Craig from Hydaburg in summers to fish, pick berries and plant potatoes. She worked at Waterfall when she was about 9 years old for 15 cents an hour. When she earned $15, she quit. "I had more money than I knew what to do with," she says.

By 1939, the island that contained Craig had been joined to Prince of Wales Island by a causeway, and was covered with houses connected by board walks.

A sawmill operated in Craig for many years and during both world wars provided high-grade spruce for use in airplane construction. Mrs. Yates' husband, Tex, opened the town's hardware store in the early 1950s. By the mid-1960s, Craig was a slowly dying fishing village. Salmon runs were poor and canneries at Steamboat Bay and Waterfall closed. Craig became a maintenance station for Columbia-Ward Fisheries, which had purchased the canneries in 1959. A new cold storage opened in 1969, beginning the town's revival.

KLAWOCK

Today the island's second largest town, Klawock is the birthplace of the Alaska salmon industry. The first salmon cannery opened here in 1878 and operated for 51 seasons.

In 1868, George Hamilton ran a trading post and salmon saltery in Klawock. He sold

Second largest town on the island, Klawock evolved from trading post and salmon saltery 125 years ago into a community that looks to seafood processing, tourism and perhaps timber processing to support its 800 residents. (Don Pitcher)

Spawning chum salmon draw gulls to Disappearance Creek on South Arm, Cholmondeley Sound, Prince of Wales Island. Eggs and milt from salmon here produced brood stock in the early 1980s for hatcheries in the Ketchikan area. (Rollo Pool)

his business to a San Francisco-based company that opened the cannery, ran a sawmill that supplied lumber for salmon packing boxes and local use, and, for a time, operated a sockeye hatchery. Other canneries operated in Klawock at various times, the last closing in the mid-1980s.

In 1993, Klawock was attempting to return to its cannery roots. Renovation of dock and cannery facilities on Bayview Avenue had

started, using more than $1 million in state and private money to reopen the facility to seafood processing.

About half of Klawock's 800 residents are Native, mostly Tlingit. The city and Native leaders want to build a major Tlingit heritage center in Klawock, to bring together the history, culture and artifacts of Tlingits who settled the west side of Prince of Wales. Construction of a long house, a traditional place of story-telling and feasting, is planned, perhaps by 1994. A totem park, with 21 restored and replicated totems from the old village of Tuxekan, occupies the hill above town. The new center may be located near the mouth of the Klawock River, where thousand-year-old fish weirs and traps can still be found in the mud.

A couple of lodges in Klawock cater to visitors, including hunters and sport fishermen. The town could be the island's gateway for more visitors, if the airport is upgraded and tour ships start using the Klawock Island Dock Co.'s deep-water port, built during the 1980s boom in Native logging for timber sorting and ship loading.

Town leaders anticipate the reopening of a defunct sawmill outside Klawock, which operated from 1973 until 1990. Weyerhauser Co., the Tacoma-based lumber giant, acquired the facility in bankruptcy proceedings and announced plans to sell the mill, said city officials. The mill's closure put 100 employees out of work, triggering a mini-recession on the island.

HYDABURG

This traditional Haida village was founded in 1911 when Klinkwan, Howkan and Kaigani villages, from the southern end of Prince of Wales, merged to get a government school. E.W. Hawkesworth, the teacher, helped the new village form a trading company to operate a store and sawmill.

In 1927, Far North Fisheries beached its floating cannery *Pioneer* in Hydaburg, where it operated for three years. A new cannery built in 1939 operated under various owners through 1965. The buildings were converted in 1971 to cold storage, which operated until the late 1980s.

About 429 people, mostly Haidas, lived here in 1993, according to the city. Hydaburg is the primary Haida village in Southeast. Most of its residents fish commercially and depend on subsistence fishing, hunting and gathering. The town's July 4th celebration is a popular event. A park above town, which overlooks Sukkwan Narrows, displays restored totem poles from the villages that joined to form Hydaburg. In the early 1990s, Haida Corp. acquired timber stands in a land swap with the federal government and will probably log its land.

OTHER COMMUNITIES OF PRINCE OF WALES

The state ferry from Ketchikan docks at Hollis, on the island's east side off Kasaan Bay. The community of 110 has a school with a public library, but no post office. The Hollis area hosted several gold mines from 1901 to

Shooting stars and buttercups brighten moist meadows in many areas of Southeast. (John Hyde)

the 1920s, supporting an area population of about 1,000. From 1953 to 1962, Hollis was Ketchikan Pulp Co.'s main logging camp. Thick stands of second-growth timber on hillsides facing the ferry terminal are pointed out by island residents to show the forest's regenerative ability after clear-cutting.

A wide, paved highway from Hollis goes west 31 miles, through mountains and valleys, to Klawock and Craig. A spur south leads to Hydaburg. Out of Klawock, a gravel road goes north some 100 miles to Labouchere Bay, a Ketchikan Pulp Co. logging camp of about 150 people on Sumner Strait.

The small fishing communities of Point Baker and Port Protection, north of

Labouchere Bay, are not connected to the road system — by choice. Separated by a few small islands and a peninsula, the communities are summer home to boats fishing Sumner Strait and the outer islands.

About 40 people live year-round in Point Baker on the island's northwesternmost tip. Named in 1793 by Capt. George Vancouver for his second lieutenant, fish buyers set up stations here in the late 1930s, and homesteaders followed. Port Protection, about two miles south with nearly 60 people, likewise has been used for years by boats seeking shelter, including Vancouver's in 1793. In 1947 at Wooden Wheel Cove, Laurel "Buckshot" Woolery built a log store. A fish-

buying station opened and a handful of fishermen built cabins.

The people of both communities are self-sufficient, heat with wood, generate their own electricity, and use boats as their local transportation. The Point Baker post office serves both communities. In good weather, they may boat to Wrangell for supplies.

The road between Labouchere Bay and Klawock branches west to Naukati Bay where Ketchikan Pulp Co. operates a logging camp of about 93 people; and east to the community of Whale Pass, with a store, lodge and about 75 people, on Whale Passage; and the towns of Coffman Cove and Thorne Bay.

Coffman Cove, one of the largest

independent logging camps in Southeast before being bought by Ketchikan Pulp Co., recently incorporated as a town. About 185 people live here, with a school, churches, grocery, several lodges and video store. The first oyster farm in Alaska, Canoe Lagoon Oysters, has been operating in Coffman Cove since about 1980.

A newly opened road to the south leads to the town of Thorne Bay, at the mouth of Thorne River. With about 570 people, it is the island's third largest town. The *Island News*, a weekly tabloid published here, covers the entire island. It carries announcements collected from three big drop-boxes in Craig and Klawock and submitted from outlying camps via floatplane.

In 1962, Ketchikan Pulp Co. moved its main logging camp to Thorne Bay from Hollis, and for years the camp was the largest in the world. In 1982, the town incorporated after state land was made available for homesites. Now Ketchikan Pulp Co.'s main sort yard is here. Wilderness lodges nearby cater to sport fishermen, particularly those angling the river's famous runs of steelhead. The community is regularly served by float-plane and barge, and a large supermarket in Ketchikan owns the local grocery. The town got a new school and gym in the early 1990s. Most people live in trailers with additions, although modern frame homes are appearing.

From Thorne Bay, a road is being extended south to secluded Kasaan, on the west side of Kasaan Peninsula. This town of about 55 includes Natives represented by Kavilco Inc. village corporation. The villagers fish, hunt, trap and gather beach foods in a year-round subsistence lifestyle.

Kasaan originated in 1898 as a copper mining camp, with a sawmill and store. A tribe of Haidas from the north shore of Skowl Arm eventually moved close to camp. Copper mining lasted about four years, but a salmon cannery opened and, despite three fires and numerous owners, operated through 1953.

Old Kasaan burned in 1918, but some of the original totems that escaped destruction are now at the Totem Heritage Center in Ketchikan. The Kasaan Totem Park stands on a point of land near the town, part of the forest service's effort in 1938 to salvage and restore abandoned totem poles. It is connected to the town and harbor by a boardwalk.

Gildersleeve Logging Inc. out of Ketchikan operates three floating logging camps on the southeast coast of the island: a 30-person camp at Dora Bay in Cholmondeley Sound; a 60-person camp in Tolstoi Bay, on the north shore of Kasaan Peninsula; and a 50-person camp in Polk Inlet off Skowl Arm.

Loggers clear-cut large tracts at Divide Head on Chomondeley Sound. Debate continues about the wisdom of clear-cutting, but especially on the north part of the island, large sections of Prince of Wales forests on both Native and national forest lands have been clear-cut. (Chip Porter)

■ Wrangell ■

Wrangell is Alaska's only city to have flown Russian, British and American flags. Furs, gold and salmon created the scrappy town. Trees and fish sustain it.

The town faces Zimovia Strait, near the north tip of Wrangell Island. Its waterfront bustles with log and ore ships, tugs, fishing boats and pleasure craft, state ferries and small tour ships. A cannery, cold storage, and two other seafood processors handle salmon, halibut, black cod, herring, shrimp and crab hauled in by Wrangell fishermen.

A sawmill — the largest single employer with 200 people — ships spruce and hemlock lumber and logs to Washington state and Asia. Cargo planes and hovercraft bring ore from a Canadian gold mine to Wrangell to be loaded on ships. Tourists visit too, although not in the numbers seen in Southeast's larger cities.

A wide main street holds downtown, mostly built after a 1952 fire destroyed the waterfront, which was rebuilt after a 1906 fire. Town extends up a wooded hillside. Here are some of Alaska's oldest institutions — the oldest Protestant church, the oldest Catholic parrish, the oldest continuously published newspaper, the *Wrangell Sentinel.* Wrangell Museum is housed in what was the state's oldest integrated school for whites and Natives.

Next door, the newly renovated city library feeds Wrangell's voracious reading appetite. The town's 2,600 residents read three times more books a year than Americans in other towns its size.

Distinct to Wrangell are dark red garnets, semiprecious stones which children often sell dockside. A garnet ledge on the Stikine River, once mined by the nation's first all-female corporation, was willed in 1962 to Wrangell's children. Parents take their kids by flat-bottomed river boat to the outcropping where they sledgehammer and chisel off garnet-studded rocks.

Wrangell youngsters with muffin tins loaded with garnets sell their wares to ferry and cruise ship passengers. The garnet ledge, located upriver in the Stikine Valley, was deeded to the children of Wrangell in 1962 by former Wrangell mayor Fred Hanford. (Don Pitcher)

The Stikine River enters Southeast six miles north of Wrangell. This 400-mile waterway out of British Columbia is Southeast's only navigable river. It figures prominently in Wrangell's past and present. The lower Stikine — part of the Stikine-LeConte Wilderness — is a playground for area residents who fish its waters, watch birds and hunt ducks and moose in its delta marshlands and valley. About 16 miles upriver, the U.S. Forest Service maintains Chief Shakes Hot Springs, a popular day trip from Wrangell.

South of Wrangell at Anan Creek on upper Cleveland Peninsula, dozens of people a day congregate at a forest service platform to watch brown and black bears feed on pink salmon during July and August.

The Stikine tribe of Tlingits first fished and hunted the area, trading shells, fish oil, and otter and seal skins for the animal hides collected by interior Indians upriver. Hudson's Bay Co., which controlled trade in Canada for England, raced to claim the Stikine, but the Russian American Co., headquartered in Sitka, arrived first and in 1834 erected Fort Dionysius.

Six years later, Russia leased mainland Southeast to the Hudson's Bay Co., who renamed the post Fort Stikine. Stikine Tlingits moved nearer, trading furs for cloth and wool blankets. A footbridge in Wrangell leads to Chief Shakes Island in the harbor, where a tribal house and aged totems commemorate the Stikines.

In 1869, the U.S. Army established Fort Wrangell. For three years, the fort presided over a few gold miners on the Stikine, some former Hudson's Bay men and the Indians.

In 1872, gold discoveries in the Cassiar district of British Columbia triggered a rush up the Stikine River. Wrangell boomed and the military returned. In 1877, a Presbyterian

mission and boarding school opened. Steamships ferried miners between Wrangell and Telegraph Creek near the gold fields. But the gold played out by decade's end, and the miners and soldiers moved on, leaving behind a small harbor village of old Indian houses and totems.

Then, like elsewhere in Southeast, salmon became big business. In 1887, Aberdeen Packing Co. opened a cannery to harvest Stikine River salmon. A lumber mill supplied wooden packing boxes.

In 1898, Wrangell pulsed from the Klondike gold rush in the Yukon as miners forged up the Stikine to the Teslin trail. But this circuitous route quickly lost favor to

The lumbering and fishing community of Wrangell, population 2,600, curves around a harbor near the northern tip of Wrangell Island. Several miles of roads lead out from town. The longest of these runs south along the west side of the island past the lumber mill; the buildings of the now-closed Wrangell Institute, a school; then cross island to a small picnic site and log loading area on Eastern Channel. (John Warden)

the passes at the head of Lynn Canal.

Wrangell's fishing industry grew in the profitable 1920s and 1930s. The town also served commercial riverboats on the Stikine.

The 1950s brought large-scale timber harvesting. Wrangell's waterfront sawmill, operating since 1888, was bought by Alaska Pulp Corp., owner of Sitka's pulp mill. The company opened a second mill outside town. In the early 1980s, the company replaced those with a new high-tech mill. Wrangell claims the title of Lumber Capital of Alaska, but that hinges on continued logging in Tongass National Forest.

Shorebirds by the thousands pass through the Stikine flats on their annual migrations. Eighty-eight to 95 percent of the shorebirds are western sandpipers; most of the remaining are dunlins. The region's second largest concentration of bald eagles gathers here when hooligan are running and an outgoing tide traps the small fish in pools. (Don Cornelius)

■ Petersburg ■

Spread over a hillside on north Mitkof Island, with Wrangell Narrows in front and muskeg meadows behind, is the town of Petersburg, population 3,680. The town today depends on fishing and seafood processing, just as it did when Peter Buschmann founded the community more than 90 years ago.

Hardy Scandinavians, mostly Norwegians, settled Petersburg. It was not a hastily assembled boom town, so its streets were neatly laid out and its homes constructed to last. Today, old buildings appear freshly painted and shops are often decorated with traditional Norwegian floral designs called rosemaling. The tidiness extends to winter snowplowing of sidewalks with square-edged paths around fire hydrants and storm water drains.

The waterfront shows the town's livelihood, with four fish processing plants, docks for fuel, barges, ships and ferries, and a large harbor for fishing boats. Petersburg rivals Sitka as the top halibut port in Southeast.

Petersburg Fisheries Inc., a division of Icicle Seafoods Inc., is a year-round operation located in a complex of white buildings on the waterfront. Part of Buschmann's original 1899-built cannery is incorporated into this modern processing plant for halibut, black cod, crab, salmon and herring. Alaska Glacier Seafoods, a division of Norquest Seafoods Inc.,

Caitlan and Annie McCabe, daughters of John and Carol McCabe of Petersburg, pose in traditional Norwegian dress for the Little Norway Festival, held annually the third weekend of May in conjunction with Norwegian Independence Day. (Karen Cornelius)

LEFT: *Because Petersburg lies at the north end of a tricky navigation channel known as the Wrangell Narrows and because the town lacks a deep-water port, large cruise ships forego calling here. But an important fishing fleet homeports at this community of 3,680. (Harry M. Walker)*

ABOVE: *The float hanging from this boat in Petersburg's harbor seems to reflect the orderliness with which this fishing community was laid out. (Don Cornelius)*

cans and freezes the famed small, high-quality Petersburg shrimp and handles crab, salmon and halibut. Nelbro Packing Co. and Chatham Strait Seafoods operate mostly seasonal salmon canneries and cold storages. At least one family-operated custom processor stays busy, too. In 1993 to better supply the seafood processors, the city was doubling capacity of its water supply with a dam on Cabin Creek, southeast of town.

Because Petersburg lacks a deep-water port, it is not visited by large cruise ships. However its location on Wrangell Narrows, one of the principal Inside Passage channels, makes Petersburg a convenient stop for smaller tour boats and the state ferry. It gets regular jet service out of Juneau.

The town's annual Little Norway Festival attracts statewide, and sometimes national, attention. Day cruises to nearby LeConte Glacier, along with driving the 34-mile Mitkof Highway south of town are local attractions. Trumpeter swans can be seen, late October through April, at an observatory on the highway at Blind Slough.

LeConte Glacier, Alaska's most southerly tidewater glacier, played a role in Petersburg's early fishing fame by providing ice for fish packers. Although established as a salmon cannery, Petersburg owes its early growth to halibut.

In 1899, Norwegian cannery pioneer Peter Buschmann interested his business associates in a cannery site near his son's homestead at what became Petersburg. Icy Straits Packing Co. began fishing for herring and halibut. Alaska's halibut fishery was virtually nonexistent at the time, but these bottom-fish were abundant in nearby Frederick Sound and Chatham Strait. They were packed in glacier ice, shipped to Seattle and East Coast markets.

The winter halibut fishery complemented summer salmon runs. More fishing families arrived, many of them Scandinavians drawn by Buschmann. A post office opened in 1900. The progressive community raised money for a hydroelectric plant in 1925 and formed the Bank of Petersburg, which remained locally owned until 1971.

Petersburg also pioneered Alaska's frozen shrimp industry. In 1916, Earl N. Ohmer and brother-in-law Karl I. Sifferman formed Alaska Glacier Seafoods to handle the distinctively flavored shrimp found within a 40-mile radius of town. They introduced trawling to catch the shrimp.

A unique part of Petersburg for 35 years was the University of Alaska's experimental fur farm started in 1937. Nearly 60 fur farms operated in the Petersburg area until fur farming in Southeast ended in 1972.

Today, Petersburg is homeport to two U.S. Coast Guard cutters. The U.S. Forest Service supervisor and district ranger offices of Tongass National Forest are located here. One small independent sawmill in Petersburg produces green lumber from small tract sales of Tongass timber off Mitkof Island.

A worker at Petersburg Fisheries Inc. stacks frozen halibut. The town rivals Sitka as the top halibut port in Southeast. (Karen Cornelius)

A Daughter of Petersburg

By Marilee Enge

Editor's note: *Marilee is a reporter for the* Anchorage Daily News.

Our airplane sat on the runway at Anchorage International. It was the day before Christmas Eve and I was on my way home to Petersburg. I was

BELOW: *A descendant of one of the first Norwegian families to settle in Petersburg, Marilee Enge explored the homeland of her ancestors in a visit to the fishing community of Ålesund, Norway, in July 1992. (Courtesy of Marilee Enge)*

RIGHT: *Marilee Enge's grandparents, Martin and Augusta Enge, built this house in Petersburg in 1929. Marilee's parents now live here. (Courtesy of Marilee Enge)*

anxious to be on my way, but it seemed there was no hurry. Snow was falling all along the Panhandle and planes weren't landing there. We made a pass at Juneau, but ended up in Sitka, a lovely town but not on the itinerary. It was the only airport north of Ketchikan that was open and Christmas passengers began to converge there.

My family had agreed to gather for the holidays, always a risky plan that time of year. Other Petersburg expatriates were stuck in the Sitka airport too. We talked about how we might get home: A chartered plane? A fishing boat? Would the jet make a run for it? Then we learned that the Alaska ferry *LeConte* was passing through and would get us home in time. We climbed aboard that evening, camped on the snowy deck and the overnight voyage ended in Petersburg on Christmas Eve — just in time for *julebukking*.

Petersburg lives for two seasons: fishing and Christmas. During the summer, people are too busy to just hang out. December, however, is set aside for visiting and eating. *Julebukking* is a custom of the Norwegians who founded Petersburg. It involves eating delicacies like pickled herring and butter cookies, drinking and swapping stories with people you might not talk to for the next 11 months. On Christmas Eve day, Main Street merchants serve food and drinks and folks walk from shop to shop getting pleasantly toasted. It's a tradition that draws the community together, and it's one reason we return.

My great-grandparents, Anna and Rasmus Enge, came to Southeast Alaska in 1901 to work for a fellow Norwegian named Peter Buschmann, who had built a salmon cannery on Mitkof Island. In Norway, Rasmus had made his living catching codfish

in the Lofoten Islands and shipping it to southern Europe. But times were tough and he and Anna followed the migration of their country folk to the American Midwest, on to Seattle and finally to Alaska. They settled there and never left. They came from a fiord-and-island region in the northwest of Norway, and in Southeast Alaska they found a kindred geography.

Buschmann hired them in Seattle and they traveled north on a steamer. A few hours after they arrived in his industrial settlement, Buschmann sent them to a new cannery location he was planning in a remote bay. It was January and they had to build a shack to live in. The weather promptly turned bitterly cold and they were iced in most of the winter, unable to replenish staples like flour and butter. They survived on venison and moved to town after the spring thaw. There they built a home and Anna became the first non-Native woman to settle in Petersburg. It was three more years before another Norwegian woman moved to town.

Besides their fishing, Rasmus and Anna were entrepreneurs. They ran a store, a restaurant, a roller skating rink and a movie theater. According to one old-timer who knew them, Rasmus liked to "get in his cups now and then," and frequently started the movie upside down. People would stamp and holler and he would give it another try. When he still didn't get it right, Anna would stomp on stage and announce, "No show tonight. Enge is drunk."

His son Martin, my grandfather, fished for salmon and halibut around

Petersburg his whole life. My father fished to put himself through the University of Washington, where he was one of the first students to graduate with a degree in fisheries. And two of my brothers still make their living fishing. Dad bought them a little wooden gillnetter named the *Gypsy* when they were in high school and they spent their summers running up and down Wrangell Narrows each week, pulling salmon from the waters of Clarence Strait and Frederick Sound.

I went aboard the *Gypsy* when I was 8 or 9. I remember sleeping on a narrow bunk, drinking Tang from mugs and peeing in a bucket on deck. The pinks were running strong that week and my brother Steve kept setting the net and pulling it in, loading the little boat until water nearly lapped over the gunwales. I finally begged him to stop fishing for fear we would sink.

I spent most of my summers working in the canneries, packing skeins of salmon roe into wooden boxes for shipment to Japan. Young girls started in the egg room because it was safer than working around canning equipment. It was a female community, supervised by a crew of domineering and exacting Japanese egg technicians. Girls who failed to shake the exact amount of salt on their layers of roe got a quick lesson from a brusque egg official who spoke little English.

The cannery was a social hub for teenage girls in the summers. All my friends worked there, and it was the best place to meet new boys. There was something about a guy from Seattle, wearing Helly Hansen oilskins and tossing salmon out of the hold of a seine boat. We lived for coffee breaks when we could gossip on the dock and watch the fishing crews pitch off.

TOP RIGHT: *Marilee, her parents, Carol and John, and her nephew Jesse take a break during an outing to pick nagoonberries on the mainland near Petersburg. John, a retired salmon cannery manager, was born in Petersburg. Carol, originally from an Iowa farm, came to town after World War II to teach fourth grade. (Courtesy of Marilee Enge)*

RIGHT: *Fishermen work on their nets along the busy waterfront at Petersburg. (Charlie Crangle)*

LEFT: *Residences and fishermen's warehouses line Hammers Slough in the older part of Petersburg. The Hammers, who came from the northwest coast of Norway, run a grocery store in town. (Courtesy of Marilee Enge)*

BOTTOM LEFT: *Carol Enge collects seaweed at Sandy Beach on the shore of Frederick Sound. She uses the seaweed as a fertilizer on her garden. (Courtesy of Marilee Enge)*

gallons on hot days, getting sun-tanned meanwhile. We'd find a cool stream to dive into when we were done. In August, we took the outboard across the Sound to pick rare and luscious nagoonberries on the mainland. Then there was the search for *moltebær*, or cloudberries, but rumor always had it that certain Norwegian ladies had picked them green. That's against the law in Norway. Finally, after the first frost, we scanned muskeg meadows for tiny *tyttebær*, or lingonberries.

Extreme low tides in the fall were time for digging clams and collecting seaweed, which my mom used to fertilize and protect her garden through the winter. My brothers would hunt for deer and ducks and blue grouse, which everyone calls "hooters."

When I was growing up winters were always colder than in recent years, and the streams and sloughs on Mitkof Island would freeze solid. On Sunday afternoons during a long, cold stretch, it seemed like half the town would drive to Blind Slough for ice skating. In my memories, the place looks like a Victorian Christmas

Island living shaped our world in lots of ways. Take The End of the Road. The "highway" system on Mitkof Island consists of one road that runs from town to a point about 30 miles south — The End of the Road. There wasn't anything to see there particularly, but it was a destination. More often, though, my family would load into the outboard and head down the Narrows or across Frederick Sound for summer outings. They usually included fishing and berry picking — a family obsession.

Bright red huckleberries that grew best on logged-off hillsides began to ripen in July. My mom made them into the world's best pies. We picked

card, with couples skating arm-in-arm, and chains of kids playing crack-the-whip on skates. There was always a bonfire and Thermoses full of hot chocolate.

I joined the swim team right after I learned how to swim in the fifth grade and ended up captain of the high school team. The smell of chlorine still gives me butterflies in my stomach. Most of my friends went on to be cheerleaders or to play volleyball, so the swim team was a small and quirky but dedicated group. We traveled by ferry to meets in other towns, and my impressions of those communities are still wrapped around swimming trips. Like walking through a Taku storm to get to the regional championships in Juneau, or our whole team hanging out on a wooden stairway that climbed up a Ketchikan hillside on a dark, rainy night.

But boys basketball is the center of Petersburg's social life, always has been. Everyone goes to the games, and the adults take it more seriously than the kids. I hear a support group was even formed recently for parents of boys who got kicked off the team. Seems like it was more fun back when I was there. The high school gym on Friday nights was the place to see and be seen. Clothes had to be just right before you stepped under the blazing lights and searched the bleachers for a place to sit. We went to every home game and the school even paid for a bunch of us to follow the team to the Southeast tournament where they would break our hearts once again.

I didn't know how unusual and protected my childhood was until I went away to college in California. I'd never been to a rock concert, never heard of Szechuan food and never read a daily newspaper. I went home with a friend for Thanksgiving and I was shocked when her uncle stripped and joined us in the hot tub.

Petersburg's a little more wordly now, too. You can even buy a capuccino there.

Sometimes it makes me sad to go back. People keep tearing down the monuments of my childhood, cutting down the deep, dark woods where we built forts, and played hide-and-seek and kissed. Many of the places that live in my memories don't exist anymore. It's jarring to walk past the spot where the old gymnasium used to be. It was a wonderful, barn-shaped place with high rafters and a polished floor where I learned to serve a volleyball and perform Norwegian folk dances and went to my first prom.

They tore it down, along with the old marineways, a vaulted structure where boats were pulled ashore for repairs. And someone built an ugly condominium complex across the back of Hammers Slough, an inlet in the middle of town with stilted warehouses and a board street that was the closest you could get to the feeling of old Petersburg. I remember pushing my sister's stroller down the walk to visit our relative, Malfrid Enge, whose house overlooks the slough. It always smelled of herring.

You don't hear much Norwegian on the street corners anymore. I miss our neighbor, Gus, who would have a few too many at the Harbor Bar and totter up the walk chatting to the dandelions. His best friend was my dog, Sam. She would sit on his porch until Gus came out and spoke to her in his sing-song Norwegian accent. A nice, young couple lives there now, but I still call it Gus' house.

At least they still go *julebukking*.

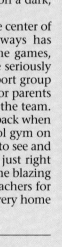

In this photo taken many years ago, the men of the Enge family gather at Petersburg Creek. From left are John, Steve, Arnold with the puppy and John Jr. (Courtesy of Marilee Enge)

■ Kupreanof ■

A short skiff ride across Wrangell Narrows from Petersburg is the tiny town of Kupreanof, on the east coast of Lindenberg Peninsula, Kupreanof Island. Formerly known as West Petersburg, Kupreanof was incorporated to preserve the independent lifestyles of its few residents, about 23 in the 1990 federal census.

The earliest settlers arrived shortly after Petersburg was founded. A small sawmill and a large mink ranch operated for a time. Mostly, Kupreanof has been a place where people could live as they wanted.

Still today, people get their water from wells or creeks and generate their own electricity. The houses are strung out along the water, some connected by boardwalks. There are no roads or cars, and people use skiffs or kayaks to get around. Some boat to work in Petersburg, where they pick up their mail and supplies, and school their children.

Petersburg tried to annex the area in the 1970s. Seeing no advantage to becoming part of the city's tax base, Kupreanof residents decided to incorporate as a second-class city in 1975.

Kupreanof adjoins the mouth of Petersburg Creek, now part of the Petersburg Creek-Duncan Salt Chuck Wilderness. Kupreanof's people supported creation of the wilderness, having already chosen rustic living in natural, uncrowded surroundings.

■ Kake ■

The Kake Indians once dominated and defended important trade routes around Kuiu and Kupreanof islands. In doing so, they clashed periodically with other Southeast tribes over hunting, fishing and trading rights. In the late 1700s and early 1800s, they also clashed with foreign explorers and traders.

As the sea otter trade slowed, the Kakes found new ways to obtain manufactured trade goods and non-Native foods. In 1857, they paddled cedar canoes south to Port Townsend, Wash., to pick inland-growing hops for wages. A Kake chief was killed there. The Kakes returned the next year and killed a customs agent in retribution, fulfilling the Tlingit custom of seeking full redress.

Tensions escalated. In 1869, a Sitka sentry shot a Native. The Kakes killed two white prospectors. The federal government dispatched the USS *Saginaw* to shell Kake villages. Landing parties smashed canoes and whatever else withstood gunfire. The Kakes escaped into the woods, but the destruction of homes, boats and food left them barely able to survive winter and they scattered to live with other tribes.

Eventually, they regrouped on the north-western tip of Kupreanof Island, a former village site. By 1891, the new village of Kake had a school. Presbyterian and Salvation Army missions arrived, and the villagers denounced Indian ways. Kake Day, on Jan. 6,

A large mink ranch once operated at Kupreanof, a tiny enclave of independent residents on the opposite shore of Wrangell Narrows from Petersburg. Inland from the settlement lies the Petersburg Creek-Duncan Salt Chuck Wilderness of Tongass National Forest. (Don Cornelius)

Kake, with its 800 residents, is showing increased interest in tourism, and renewed interest in Tlingit culture. A tourism campaign is centered on a historic salmon cannery on the town's waterfront. Tlingit traditions are being resurrected with classes in traditional dance and language, clothes making, and preparation of foods such as seal flippers, fish heads and bear meat. (Don Cornelius)

commemorates the 1912 ceremony when villagers drove a silver stake, to nail shut "witchcraft, superstitions and other dark things." About this time many villagers burned totem poles and dance regalia. Thus, Kake became the first Native village to incorporate, gaining its people U.S. citizenship.

Today, Kake is a modern community of about 800, mostly Tlingit people. The town gets regularly scheduled flights from Juneau and Petersburg; the ferry stops weekly.

Kake Tribal Corp. operates a cold storage facility that buys salmon and halibut from local fishermen. The regional and village corporations do logging nearby, although first-growth harvest is nearly finished on

village corporation land. Berry bushes and stumps flank town where the forest once stood. Most villagers fish, hunt and gather natural foods to supplement commercial fishing, logging, clerking and office jobs.

The village corporation and the Organized Village of Kake tribal council are promoting Kake to tourists, for its sportfishing, moderate rainfall and Native culture, including a totem reputed to be the world's tallest at 132.5 feet.

The tourism centerpiece is the town's old salmon cannery, a complex of waterfront buildings built in 1912. The cannery is unique to Southeast with its original buildings and turn-of-the-century equipment. It operated until the mid-1980s and is being nominated to the National Register of Historic Places. A bunkhouse is being renovated into a 10-room lodge. About 20 local fishermen are training for charter boat operator licenses.

A cultural renaissance also grips Kake. The Keex' Kwaan (People of Kake) Dancers formed in 1988, part of a movement to preserve language and traditions known by a shrinking number of village elders. People meet weekly to make dance blankets and other regalia. Children learn the Native language at school. In summer, a week-long cultural camp teaches basic skills of drying salmon, preserving berries and rendering seal grease, along with more obscure traditions such as smoking bear meat, roasting seal flippers and fermenting fish heads. The dancers and camp are partly funded by the state's suicide prevention program, to encourage sobriety through drug- and alcohol-free activities.

Andy Taylor and Dave Doyon display a brace of ducks, mostly mallards, they hunted on Kupreanof Island, site of the community of Kake. (Chip Porter)

Baranof and ■ Chichagof Islands ■

Baranof and Chichagof islands appear at a glance to be one, so narrow is the zigzagging waterway, Peril Strait, that severs the two.

Together these islands resemble an arrowhead pointing south. Storms off the Pacific Ocean lash their western coasts. Long narrow waterways fracture their shorelines. On Chichagof, inlets practically pinch the island into four pieces.

A mountainous spine bisects Baranof's length. Rising sharply from sea level, the peaks reach heights of 4,600 feet with expansive snowfields on northern Baranof.

The islands are part of Tongass National Forest. Trees cover more than half the land. Most of the cut timber goes to Alaska Pulp Corp. mills in Sitka and Wrangell. The South Baranof Wilderness, the Pleasant-Lemesurier-Inian Islands Wilderness, the West Chichagof-Yakobi Wilderness, and some 300,000 acres of roadless lands on Chichagof were designated by Congress to mitigate logging.

The U.S. Forest Service maintains 18 remote cabins on these islands and neighboring Yakobi and Kruzof islands.

The yacht Tsarina *anchors in calm waters in a narrow inlet on the west coast of Chichagof Island. Hot mineral springs bubble to the surface at several locations on Baranof and Chichagof islands. Goddard Hot Springs, on Baranof's coast 16 miles south of Sitka, may have been the earliest Alaska mineral springs known to Europeans. Today, it is owned by the city of Sitka, which maintains two sheltered wooden tubs. At White Sulphur Hot Springs, in the West Chichagof-Yakobi Wilderness, a natural rock basin holds water piped from nearby springs. (R.E. Johnson)*

Fishing, hunting, boating, flight-seeing and watching wildlife are popular recreations. Boaters can reach hot springs overlooking the ocean at several locations, including Goddard Hot Springs south of Sitka and White Sulphur Hot Springs in the West Chichagof-Yakobi Wilderness.

The historic town of Sitka, on Baranof's west coast, prospers as a fishing, tourism and educational center for the region.

Here, briefly, are the other communities of Baranof and Chichagof.

The quiet hamlet of Port Alexander, on Baranof's southern tip five miles northeast of Cape Ommaney, once hosted nearly 1,000 fishing boats trolling Chatham Strait. A fish buying station and salmon packer opened in 1918. Within four years, the community included five stores, two bakeries, four restaurants, several bars and "amusement houses." For a time, a herring reduction plant operated at Port Armstrong, three miles north. As salmon runs declined in the 1950s, Port Alexander faded.

A government land sale in the 1970s brought new homesteaders, and Port Alexander incorporated in 1974.

About 120 people, mostly commercial fishermen, live here today. Most reside across the bay from old town, with its school, post office and floatplane dock. A local message program airs daily over CB radio. People get around by skiffs and kayaks, and a "school boat" meets the children each morning on the beach. Mail and groceries arrive three times a week by plane, weather permitting. Port Alexander averages about 168 inches of rain a year, making it one of the wetter Southeast towns.

One of the state's all-time rainiest spots is a few miles north along Baranof's east coast at Little Port Walter. A salmon research facility here is tended year-round by caretakers.

Baranof, in Warm Springs Bay on the east coast opposite Sitka, is home to a few commercial fishermen.

Tenakee Springs, a one-street town of about 100 people on east Chichagof, is best known for its hot springs. The gushing mineral water attracted miners as a wintering spot in the late 1800s. Today, the springs are the community's central bath and draw visitors seeking a rustic getaway. The town has two cafes, a general store built in 1899, and boat and cabin rentals.

The springs are inside an antiquated bathhouse off the dock. The outer changing room has wooden benches; the inner room contains the springs, in a deep concrete tub. Times for men's and women's use are posted on the door.

In its early years, Tenakee Springs was rowdy with bars and gambling joints. Canneries opened nearby in the early 1900s. Today, residents are mostly retirees and young families wanting a quiet life. Juneau and Sitka residents keep summer homes here, also.

Across Tenakee Inlet from town is the logging camp of Corner Bay. Another logging camp is at Kennel Creek, off Freshwater Bay.

The Tlingit village of Hoonah, population 800, sits on Chichagof's northeast coast near the mouth of Port Frederick. Tlingit legend tells of people from Glacier Bay settling this "place where the north wind doesn't blow" during the last ice age.

Hoonah fishermen from early times caught salmon and halibut in Icy Strait. Even today, Native carvers make large wooden halibut hooks, artful replicas of traditional tools. During the profitable fur trading years, Hoonah men excelled in sea otter and seal hunting. The Presbyterian mission arrived in the 1880s; today seven denominations have churches here.

Salmon canneries in the early 1900s

TOP LEFT: *Fifteen to 20 minutes by air from Juneau lies the logging and fishing town of Hoonah, population about 800, on the east shore of Port Frederick. Much of the Hoonah village corporation land has been logged. As that industry phases out, Hoonah officials are considering tourism as an additional pillar in the town's economy. (Don Pitcher)*

LEFT: *Ruffled waters of the Pacific Ocean hit the southwest tip of Chichagof Island at Salisbury Sound. Kakul and Sergius narrows connect Salisbury Sound with Peril Strait. Combined, these passages separate Baranof from Chichagof Island. (Kent Wranic)*

spurred commercial fishing. Now a privately owned cold storage in town buys salmon, halibut, crab and black cod. Some fishermen sell to Excursion Inlet Packing across Icy Strait. Hoonah's fishermen worry about remaining competitive in this highly politicized industry increasingly dominated by larger boats.

Yet the modern harbor and businesses — boat builders, welders, mechanics — draw a growing number of non-local fishermen and sport fishing charters. With its lodge, stores and other conveniences, including the school's swimming pool, Hoonah is popular with boaters awaiting permits for Glacier Bay National Park, 20 miles north.

The Tlingit culture persists. Traditional subsistence activities continue year-round. The native language is still spoken. The noted Mount Fairweather Dancers perform regularly, and local artists produce beadwork, sewing and carving.

Hoonah has not courted tourism, although that may change as logging ends on northern Chichagof within the next few years. During the past decade, logging and stevedoring of log ships provided considerable work. The U.S. Forest Service maintains a large district office here. The dock is being expanded for larger state ferries; the airstrip upgraded for larger planes. Hoonah is three hours by ferry and 15 minutes by air from Juneau.

Five miles west of Hoonah is Game Creek, an agricultural community of about 60

Steep slopes, and forests interspersed with muskeg characterize much of interior Baranof and Chichagof islands. Here moss drapes from a scattered stand of shore pine, a variety of lodgepole pine, on Baranof Island. (Bill Sherwonit)

81

FACING PAGE: *A youngster paddles around in the outer harbor at Elfin Cove, which during the summer season shelters floathouses, fishing boats and fish buying scows. (Chip Porter)*

RIGHT: *In the 1980s, Pelican, on the eastern shore of Lisianski Inlet, expanded its boat harbor and ferry dock to better accommodate boat traffic on the inlet, which trends northwest to southeast for 25 miles. Before reaching Pelican, a branch shoots southwestward off the inlet to become Lisianski Strait. The two waterways separate Yakobi Island from much larger Chichagof. (Chip Porter)*

people. Game Creek was settled in 1975 by members of the Mount Bether Bible Center.

Another Southeast fishing harbor is Elfin Cove, a community of 60 people in a sheltered bay on north Chichagof. Commercial fishermen pack its flask-shaped harbor in summer, selling more than 2 million pounds a year to several fish buyers.

In recent years, sport fishing has blossomed with several lodges catering mostly to stateside visitors. Some in Elfin Cove want more development; others want to chain the harbor closed, says one local. Wildlife viewing and sightseeing charters operate, too. Nearby attractions include Glacier Bay; Port Althorp brown bear viewing area; the abandoned Port Althorp cannery; and World War II gun emplacements.

Originally, Elfin Cove was called "Gunkhole" — fishing lingo for any protected spot with a narrow opening to the sea. Its location near Fairweather Grounds, the largest salmon fishing banks in Southeast, made it a natural gathering place for fishermen. The first salmon packer ran a short-lived floating operation in 1927. Ernie Swanson, a fish buyer who farmed foxes on nearby Three Hill Island, then moved in. Swanson's wife, Ruth, renamed the cove Elfin. She wanted a more pleasing name than Gunkhole when she requested it be made a postal station, and picked Elfin out of the dictionary.

As summers are busy, winters are quiet. Villagers fish between storms and most fly south for a long vacation. The community's school had 12 students in 1993. Floatplanes fly scheduled service into Elfin Cove from Juneau. The state ferry passes but does not stop: "We like to say we can hit it with a snowball," says Bob Mourant, owner of Elfin Cove Travel.

The ferry does stop down around the bend in Pelican, a larger fishing town on Lisianski Inlet. Pelican, with about 265 people, is busiest in summer although its cold storage plant operates year-round, processing salmon, halibut, herring, crab and black cod.

Pelican stands on piers over the water, at the foot of a steep, forested mountain. A store, several cafes, a bed and breakfast, steam bath and small library are among the buildings lining a central boardwalk. Rosie's Bar and Grill, its bar top carved with hundreds of names, is a popular gathering place.

Pelican is also nearest town to the West Chichagof-Yakobi Wilderness, a kayaking paradise with miles of rugged coastline and inland waterways.

Kalle Raatikainen, a fish buyer out of Sitka who worked the west coast of Chichagof, founded Pelican in 1938. He wanted to build a cold storage plant closer to the fishing grounds, and chose this scenic site for its protected, deep harbor. He named the town after his boat, the *Pelican*.

■ Sitka ■

Low tides reveal a wide beach adjoining downtown Sitka where people jog, walk and sit on boulders and driftwood logs. It is a good place to watch crimson sunsets sneak across the sky. Boats chug through island-dotted Sitka Sound, which empties into the Pacific Ocean. On the sound's western edge looms snow-covered Mount Edgecumbe, a 3,201-foot dormant volcano and one of Southeast's most familiar landmarks.

Much of Alaska's history radiated from this waterfront, first occupied by Kiksadi Tlingits who called their village Shee Atika. The Russians came, then the Americans, to make Sitka their Alaska capital. Today, this Baranof Island city of 8,588 people is a regional education, medical and commercial center. It is one of Southeast's biggest and busiest fishing ports.

Unlike many other Southeast towns dominated by fishing and timber, Sitka is diversified with a private college, a state university branch, a Native boarding school, a U.S. Coast Guard base, two hospitals and the senior citizens' Pioneer Home. A raptor rehabilitation center handles injured birds from throughout the region. And tourism is big. Sitka's Russian legacy, Native culture, sport fishing and wildlife viewing help make it one of Southeast's most visited towns.

The Russians first came in 1741. Alexei Chirikov, part of Vitus Bering's expedition, sailed into what is assumed to be Sitka Sound. But his two landing parties disappeared without a trace. In 1799, Alexander Baranov, chief manager of the Russian-American Co., returned with Aleut sea otter hunters and built a trading post. Local Tlingits traded pelts for guns, powder, lead and whiskey. In 1802 during Baranov's absence, they attacked and destroyed the fort. Today a state campground marks this site six miles north of town.

Baranov returned in 1804 with a warship. The Kiksadi fought from a fortification on Indian River south of their village. After a week of bombardment, they retreated into the mountains. Today, the beachfront battleground is part of Sitka National Historical Park. Trails lead through giant spruce trees to the site; they are lined with totem poles from abandoned Tlingit and Haida villages on Prince of Wales Island. Today, Native artists work inside the park's interpretative center.

Russia's *Nova Arkhangelsk*, as Sitka was called, grew into the first big city along the North Pacific's west coast. This "Paris of the Pacific" boasted a library, cathedral, shipyard, brickyards, tanneries, foundry, gardens and

This house on Kogwanton Street in Sitka's Indian Village belongs to Boyd Didrickson, a 49-year-old Tlingit carver and sea otter hunter. The house is covered with 25 yellow cedar plaques carved and painted with Tlingit designs. Didrickson says another five are needed to finish the house. Didrickson and several artist friends carved some of the first panels to cover the living room ceiling of a round house he built in Juneau. When he moved back to his hometown of Sitka, he brought the panels and installed them on the outside of this house. (Harry M. Walker)

an ice farm. The Russian governor's house overlooked the harbor from Castle Hill. The Natives lived outside city walls.

Today, a walk through town passes Russian reminders. Castle Hill, with its stone walls and cannons, still provides a waterfront vista. America's 1867 purchase of Alaska was formalized here in a flag-changing ceremony. A festival each October commemorates the event.

A few blocks away, a replicated Russian blockhouse tops a knoll above a crowded neighborhood of small homes, formerly the Native settlement outside the stockade. Tlingit designs decorate the outside of a few houses.

The restored log Bishop's House, part of the national historical park, hints at the grand life the Russians attempted in Sitka. Built in 1842, it was residence, office and private chapel for Father Ioann Veniaminov, first Bishop of Alaska and now St. Innocent. In the center of downtown stands St. Michael's Cathedral, a replica of the original Russian Orthodox cathedral built in 1848. It burned in 1966, but most vestments, eucharistic vessels and icons were saved.

Downtown merchants still trade on the Russian legacy, and one store specializes in authentic Russian goods. Not all respond respectfully to reminders of the city's Russian past; the night before a statute of Baranov was to be dedicated at the Centennial Building on the waterfront, someone broke off his nose.

During the first years of American rule, some fur trading continued and prospectors found the first gold in Southeast near town at Silver Bay. But fishing crowned American success in Sitka. In 1878, one of the first two salmon canneries in Alaska opened here. The advent of gasoline engines and refrigeration propelled Sitka as the base for outer coastal fisheries in the early 1900s.

RIGHT: *The Right Reverend Bishop Gregory Afonsky views the Sitka Madonna at St. Michael's Cathedral. Originally from Kiev in the Ukraine, the Bishop came to Alaska in 1973 after being a priest in Portland, Ore. He is the first bishop to have been consecrated in Alaska, and in May 1993 celebrated his 20th anniversary as bishop, the longest tenure of any of Alaska's Russian Orthodox bishops. (Ernest Manewal)*

BELOW: *New Archangel Dancers, a favorite of visitors to Sitka, perform year-round, with increased shows during the May to September cruise ship season. Consisting of about 30 dancers, the group wears authentic costumes and performs dances from Russia, Ukraine, Moldavia, Belarus and other former Soviet republics. A non-profit organization manages the troop, and arranges for workshops at which renowned folk dance instructors teach new dances. (John Warden)*

LEFT: *Sitka has among the largest number of boat berths of any Southeast city with 1,150 spread out in several harbors. About 50 percent of the berths go to fishing boats. (Rex Melton)*

ABOVE: *Louie, a Tlingit Indian and lifelong Sitka resident, brings in a load of herring eggs. The eggs are eaten plain or boiled and dipped in seal grease. (Dan Evans)*

In 1884, Sitka became Alaska's territorial capital. The Sitka Industrial and Training School opened to teach Natives classroom subjects and trades, like carpentry and shipbuilding. The school evolved into Sheldon Jackson College, a two-year private institution operated today by the United Presbyterian Church. The Sheldon Jackson Museum houses an outstanding collection of Eskimo and Indian items from Dr. Sheldon Jackson's missionary travels across Alaska in the 1880s.

World War II brought another small boom. The U.S. Navy built a large base on nearby Japonski Island, created by connecting three smaller islands. After the war, Mount Edgecumbe High School, a boarding school for Natives opened in former Navy facilities. The school, the only state-operated boarding high school in Alaska, is known for its quality education and innovative programs.

Today, Sitka continues as a leading fishing port. Its harbors are undergoing expansion; in 1992, fishing boats occupied more than half the 1,150 berths. Two major and several smaller seafood processors handle salmon, herring, halibut and shellfish. The students at Mount Edgecumbe even run a smoked-fish business, selling their product to Japan.

A quiet, and historic, component of Sitka is its medical facilities. Alaska's first hospital was built here during Russian times. Today health care accounts for one of every nine jobs in town.

The largest private business, Alaska Pulp Corp., employs about 400 people in its mill

ABOVE: *Tom Dyehouse holds Buddy, a young eagle that has not yet attained his adult plumage and has imprinted on humans. Raptor center staff try to keep the number of humans that can handle a particular animal to a minimum to avoid confusing the animals. (John Warden)*

RIGHT: *Fresh snow and a calm morning cast a ghostly sheen on Blue Lake. A dam on the lake provides power to the Alaska Pulp Corp. mill. (Dan Evans)*

with additional jobs in logging. Its number of jobs and high pay make it one of the most important industries in the city.

Sitka cultivates a genteel air. A wide park strip with walkways, benches and tennis courts edges a modern downtown harbor. Well-kept older homes, historic buildings and the college campus with its rolling lawns flank the waterfront. Russian-style and Tlingit dance groups perform for tourists. Summers bring nationally known musicians and authors to conduct classical music series, writer's conferences and fine arts camps. Salmon and halibut derbies and the All-Alaska Logging Championship complete the fun.

■ Admiralty Island ■

Superlatives describe 100-mile-long Admiralty Island: Southeast's largest expanse of old-growth forest, the most nesting bald eagles, one of the densest populations of brown bears. The Tlingits call their ancestral home Kootznoowoo, "Fortress of the Bears."

Tongass National Forest covers most of Admiralty. All but the island's northern tip is Admiralty Island National Monument and Wilderness, off limits to logging. Admiralty's thick forests and numerous waterways support a variety of wildlife.

The best known are its 1,700 brown bears, about one per square mile. At Pack Creek, off Seymour Canal on Admiralty's east side, the state and U.S. Forest Service jointly manage a bear viewing area. More than 1,000 people visited in summer 1992, with free permits from the forest service in Juneau. The Pack Creek sanctuary is part of two areas on Admiralty closed to bear hunting.

Eagles' nests fringe Admiralty, about 900 nests in 1992. The eagles nest in old-growth spruce and hemlock trees within 200 yards of shore, close to good fishing.

Human habitation goes back at least 3,500 years, and likely earlier. Tlingit stories tell of six permanent winter villages. Capt. George Vancouver landed in 1794 at Point

---

A cross-island water trail entices canoeists and kayakers to Admiralty Island's forested wilderness. Shortly after the Ice Age, rising sea waters severed Admiralty into two main islands and several smaller ones. The current canoe trail generally follows the lowland between the two main prehistoric islands, terminating today in Mole Harbor on the east and Mitchell Bay on the west. (Pat Costello)

Retreat. Russians mined coal a short time at Mitchell Bay. During the early 1900s, the coastline buzzed with fox farms, salmon canneries, whaling stations, gold mines and logging camps. The Greens Creek mine operated on northern Admiralty from 1989 to early 1993, when low silver prices precipitated its closure.

ANGOON

The Tlingit village of Angoon, Admiralty Island's only town, sits on a low, narrow peninsula between Chatham Strait and Kootznahoo Inlet. Old clan houses line the beach, connected by dirt roads to modern homes on the hill behind.

Most of Angoon's 700 residents are Tlingit. Cultural traditions persist, including fall pay-back parties or potlatches. Commercial fishing provides cash to supplement subsistence lifestyles. Smokehouses scattered about town contain racks of fish, seal or venison bathing in alderwood smoke.

The island's population of brown bears means Angoon gets its share. Villagers warn of bears at the ball field or other places in town over CB radio, the main method of local communication.

Angoon's one store tries to meet villagers' needs. For a change of scenery or to shop for items not locally available, people go to Juneau or Sitka — six to 10 hours by ferry or an hour by floatplane.

Admiralty's scenery and wildlife present Angoon with tourism opportunities. Two nearby wilderness lodges draw hundreds of

TOP RIGHT: *Admiralty Island's only community, Angoon, population 700, lines a narrow peninsula between Chatham Strait and Kootznahoo Inlet. (Harry M. Walker)*

ABOVE: *Born in 1909 in Killisnoo, Mary John of Angoon, widowed since 1981 and the mother of 14 children, seven still living, is a member of the Raven clan. She worked in canneries at Chatham and Hood Bay, and used to run the movie house in Angoon before television came to the community. Mary is known locally as the "Rock Lady" because she picks up rocks, decorates them and gives them to friends and visitors. (Don Pitcher)*

clients a year, and some locals guide. Yet the community values its privacy, evidenced by its rejection in 1984 of state plans to build an airstrip for wheeled planes.

Angoon was established when Tlingits following a beaver noted the site's ideal location for a village. A mile to the south were other villages, including one known as Killisnoo. Angoon experienced gunboat diplomacy early in Alaska's American period.

In 1882, an Angoon medicine man was killed by an exploding whaling gun. The family demanded retribution of 200 blankets, but the Northwest Trading Co. on nearby Killisnoo Island refused. Fearing an uprising, the military in Sitka sent a revenue cutter that fired its cannon on Angoon, destroying 18 houses and 40 canoes. Six children died from smoke inhalation. In 1973, the government paid $90,000 in compensation.

As early as the 1920s, forest industry interests looked to the thick spruce and hemlock forests of Admiralty to supply their mills. But economics and timely intervention by environmentalists staved off wholesale logging on the island. With the 1980 Alaska National Interest Lands Conservation Act, much of the island became designated wilderness within Tongass National Forest. Clear-cutting has occurred in a few areas, however, and sections of the northern part of the island are open to mining and other development. (George Wuerthner)

■ Juneau ■

Gold brought people to Juneau, and with the people came government. Today government drives Juneau, Alaska's capital and Southeast's largest city. Every other job is in government.

Yet Juneau, the state's third largest city with modern office buildings, restaurants, art galleries, museums, a university and endless political brokering, is close to the edge. It is but minutes from mountain wilds and secluded saltwater fiords.

The city sprawls against Mount Roberts (3,819 feet) and Mount Juneau (3,576 feet). To the east beyond them lies the Juneau Icefield, which spawns all the area's glaciers.

The city faces Gastineau Channel on the west, its tidal link to the Inside Passage.

Downtown Juneau climbs the mountainsides, its Victorian homes reached by steep, wooden staircases from narrow streets. Historic hotels and storefronts recall Juneau's days as a mining town. Newer buildings crowd in, practically obscuring some of the oldest like St. Nicholas Russian Orthodox Church, in continuous use since 1894. Sculptures, murals and totems scattered about downtown speak to the area's Tlingit heritage. Talk in Juneau's bistros veers from the latest legislative scandal, to a controversial proposal to reopen the Alaska-Juneau (A-J) mine near downtown, to the best way to kill algae in boat fuel tanks.

The city, population nearly 29,000, spills north along the coast, lining a narrow shelf of land with shopping centers, business parks and residential suburbs. Many people live in Mendenhall Valley, 12 miles north of downtown. Tracts of houses occupy a plain gouged bare by still-receding Mendenhall Glacier. This is Southeast's only glacier accessible by car, and a U.S. Forest Service visitor's center offers a fine overview.

The road continues to Echo Cove, 40 miles north. It passes Auke Bay, site of the state ferry terminal and the University of Alaska Southeast campus. The Auk tribe of Tlingits lived here long before there was a Juneau.

Across the channel on Douglas Island is the community of Douglas, linked to

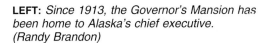

LEFT: *Since 1913, the Governor's Mansion has been home to Alaska's chief executive. (Randy Brandon)*

BELOW: *Juneau is accessible only by boat and plane. Before air transportation became common, vessels of the Alaska Steamship Co. and other lines were the main carrier of people and goods to Alaska's coastal towns. In this photo taken in 1939, the Alaska Steam vessel* Yukon *calls at Juneau. (Peter Vogel, M.D.)*

downtown by the Douglas Bridge. Once a separate town larger than Juneau during the mining peak, Douglas is now a bedroom community. Its independent and loyal following never cottoned to the city's idea of calling it "West Juneau."

Douglas is home to nationally acclaimed Perseverance Theater. The island has Southeast's only alpine ski resort, Eaglecrest. Juneau skier Hilary Lindh, silver medalist in women's downhill at the 1992 Winter Olympics, trained here.

There are almost as many cars in Juneau as residents. Yet the only way to drive here is aboard a state ferry. Studies of building a road to Haines or into Canada continue. For now, legislators fly or boat to work and convene with their constituents by teleconference. In 1976, Alaskans voted to move the capital to Willow, 65 miles north of Anchorage. They reversed the decision in 1982 because of the move's estimated cost of $2.8 billion.

Juneauites shudder at the possibility. State government alone is bigger in Juneau than the entire Alaska forest industry, and five times bigger than Southeast's tourism trade. The marble-pillared state Capitol with its five floors of offices and tiny legislative chambers is one of nearly a dozen buildings housing state and federal agencies.

But Juneau's history, accessible wilderness and cosmopolitan flair draw the tourists, about 300,000 a year. In 1992, nearly 270,000 people on 30 cruise ships visited town. More are anticipated in 1993, with one of the major cruise ship lines boosting its Southeast capacity 35 percent.

They find plenty to do. The Alaska State Museum — its eagle tree alone worth the stop — offers displays of Alaska's Native peoples, and natural and political history. The House of Wickersham houses memorabilia of Judge James Wickersham, one of Alaska's early judges and politicians. The city museum exhibits the area's mining history. Live concerts in summer fill the downtown with music, and the infrequent sunny days bring everyone outdoors.

But rain — 92 inches a year downtown and 54 inches at the airport, 10 miles north — rarely douses summer activities. Locals, crazy about softball, play even when its pouring.

Charter planes and boats reach beyond the city for wilderness and glacier tours and sport fishing. One outfitter conducts sea kayaking adventures. Trails radiate from Juneau, some reaching the ruins of some of the area's numerous mines.

Naturalist John Muir noted promising mineralization along Gastineau Channel in 1879. In 1880, Sitka mining engineer George Pilz sent prospectors Joseph Juneau and Richard Harris to the area. They followed a Tlingit named Kowee up Gold Creek to some of the richest gold-bearing ground in the Juneau Gold Belt. Within a year, nearly 300 miners had reached the settlement of Juneau at the creek's mouth.

Nearly half a dozen mines, including the A-J, the world's largest, contributed to the town's rapid growth. Alaska's first political convention was held here in summer 1881, and the city incorporated in 1900. As more people arrived, the capital was transferred from Sitka, a two-year process completed in 1906.

BELOW: *An employee of Alaskan Brewing Co. checks the production line at the company's Juneau brewery. The company, founded in 1986, bases its beverage on a turn-of-the-century Douglas City Brewing Co. recipe for Alaskan Amber. At the Great American Beer Festival in 1988, the modern-day Alaskan Amber was voted the country's best beer. (Mark Wayne)*

RIGHT: *Cross-country skiers make the short run across the ice of Mendenhall Lake to the base of Mendenhall Glacier, accessible by a short drive north of Juneau. (R.E. Johnson)*

A lode discovered in 1880 on Douglas Island developed into the mines of the Alaska Treadwell Gold Mining Co. At their peak, the four Treadwell mills dropped 960 stamps and employed 2,000 men. From this came the town of Douglas. A disastrous mine cave-in took most of the Treadwell complex in 1917. Douglas shrank as most everyone left. A 1926 fire finished off the small remaining mine, and Douglas became a Juneau suburb.

Mining ended in 1944 when the A-J closed, due to labor shortages and government insistence on higher wages during World War II. Ruins of its stamp mill stand on the hillside above Gastineau Channel near downtown. Canadian-based Echo Bay Mines Ltd. was in the permitting process in 1993 to reopen the A-J. Supporters say Juneau needs the economic diversity; others argue against mining for environmental and aesthetic reasons.

The Greens Creek mine on Admiralty Island brought returned mining to the area in 1989. Its highly-paid workers lived in Juneau, and the mine's closure in early 1993 was keenly felt.

For a time in Juneau, commercial halibut and salmon fishing were important. A sawmill and at least 11 salmon canneries operated between 1900 and 1920. Today several hatcheries operate here, but only one processor and a small commercial fleet. But four harbors serve pleasure craft, and sport fishing ranks with softball as one of Juneau's most popular summer pastimes.

Sealaska Regional Corporation

Alaska Natives are the largest private landowners in Southeast with more than 600,000 acres allotted through the Alaska Native Claims Settlement Act (ANCSA) of 1971. ANCSA granted 40 million acres of land and nearly $1 billion to the state's Natives to resolve land ownership disputes. The act created 13 regional for-profit corporations, and numerous village and urban corporations.

Southeast has one regional corporation, two urban and 10 village corporations.

The regional Sealaska Corp. represents 15,700 shareholders. It owns 340,000 acres of timber and subsurface rights to 600,000 acres.

Sealaska's businesses include exporting spruce, hemlock and red cedar logs to Asia and selling pulp logs to mills in Southeast, British Columbia and the Pacific Northwest. It projects annual harvests of 100 million board feet until about year 2003. Thinning second-growth stands will yield about 30 million board feet a year of pulp logs, starting in 1993.

Sealaska operates rock, sand and gravel quarries. It plans to quarry chemical-grade limestone on northeast Dall Island by 1995, and may develop precious and base metals mines on Prince of Wales Island in the next decade. In 1993, Sealaska was working to get community allocations included in a newly instituted individual fisheries quota program for halibut and black cod. Sealaska also manages more than $150 million in investment funds.

The corporation has returned profits to shareholders since 1985, with net earnings of more than $20 million against $100 million in gross revenues. Yearly dividends range from $500 to $1,000, with larger amounts some years.

Most Sealaska shareholders are stockholders in an urban or village corporation. The two urban corporations are Gold Belt Inc., representing Juneau; and Shee Atika Inc., for Sitka.

The village corporations are Cape Fox, Saxman; Haida Corp., Hydaburg; Huna Totem Corp., Hoonah; Kake Tribal Corp., Kake; Kavilco Inc., Kasaan; Klawock Heenya Corp., Klawock; Klukwan Inc., Klukwan; Kootznoowoo Inc., Angoon; Shaan Seet Inc., Craig; and Yak-Tat Kwaan Inc., Yakutat. These corporations collectively own 286,400 acres of mostly timberland. Each village corporation got 23,040 acres under ANCSA. Gold Belt received more than 30,000 acres and Shee Atika got more than 26,000 acres. Most of these corporations have logged all or part of their lands at a rate of about 50 million board feet a year. First-growth harvest is expected to end by about 1995. Shee Atika and Cape Fox each built a hotel, as well.

In the meantime, some 3,600 Sealaska shareholders from the communities of Ketchikan, Petersburg, Wrangell, Tenakee Springs and Haines were denied under ANCSA formation of village or urban corporations. In 1988, they formed the non-profit Southeast Alaska Land Acquisition Coalition Inc. to seek redress. In 1993, a Congressional study of their claims was underway.

Land claims by Alaska Natives date back to the first lawsuit against the federal government filed by Tlingits and Haidas. In 1936, they filed an $80 million claim for lands taken for Tongass National Forest. In 1968, a court finally awarded judgment of $7,546,053.

Today, the Tlingit-Haida Central Council, which formed in 1966 during that case, administers state and federal social and educational programs for Southeast Natives. The Tlingit-Haida Regional Housing Authority administers large federal housing grants, and the Tlingit-Haida Electrical Authority provides services under the federal rural electrification program.

A private organization, the Alaska Native Brotherhood, formed in 1912 to prepare Natives for citizenship, today represents Natives on social and economic issues.

A forester cuts a snag on Native land at View Cove on Dall Island. (Don Cornelius)

■ Lynn Canal ■

North of Juneau, Lynn Canal cuts between the Chilkat Range and the Coast Mountains. This 60-mile-long waterway, one of the continent's deepest fiords, reaches depths of 2,400 feet on its southern end.

On its northern end, Lynn Canal splits around Chilkat Peninsula into Chilkat and Chilkoot inlets, each fed by rivers. The scenery and vegetation of the Chilkat River valley shows the transition between coastal maritime and interior climates.

The town of Haines, near the head of the peninsula, faces Chilkoot Inlet near its diversion into Lutak and Taiya inlets. At the head of steep-sided Taiya Inlet is the town of Skagway. With roads to the continental highways, Skagway and Haines are important overland gateways into Southeast. State ferries serve each town.

The river valleys and mountain passes of upper Lynn Canal long provided passage through the region's otherwise largely im-penetrable geography. Chilkat and Chilkoot Indians traded along these routes to the interior ages before whites appeared. When gold discoveries in the late 1800s brought prospectors, the Indians turned their trade monopoly into a lucrative packing business.

Of the five Indian villages then, only Klukwan remains. About 130 people, mostly Chilkats, live in this traditional Chilkat River village. From Klukwan, "mother town," came master carvers and weavers; their trademark, the Chilkat blanket of mountain goat wool and cedar bark.

Carvings from Klukwan's Whale House, a clan house, are considered peerless examples of Northwest Coast Indian art. Of these, four house posts and a screen sit in a Seattle warehouse awaiting a court settlement. Whale clan members plan to sell the heirlooms; the village council wants them back.

The area's biggest draw, the Alaska Chilkat Bald Eagle Preserve, stretches north and south of Klukwan along the braided Chilkat River. Hundreds of eagles feed here each winter on late salmon runs. More than 3,500 eagles congregate during November and December's peak. Hordes of people come to watch the spectacle, easily seen just north of Haines from highway turnouts.

Haines, the largest town on Lynn Canal with 1,265 people, started as a Presbyterian mission in 1881. Gold mining, agriculture, timber and fishing played in its makeup. Its sawmill closed in 1990; now fishing on Lynn

FACING PAGE: *Thirty miles south of Haines in Lynn Canal sits Eldred Rock Light Station, the oldest original lighthouse in Alaska that is still standing. Operational on June 1, 1906, Eldred Rock Light was the last major station to be put in service during the push for lighthouse construction in the first decade of the 20th century. (Harry M. Walker)*

RIGHT: *One of Southeast's biggest salmon fleets homeports at Haines, population 1,265, site of a former Presbyterian mission that has grown into a multifaceted community. Haines relies on services, tourism, movie-making, fishing, agriculture, timber and mining to sustain its economy. (John Warden)*

ABOVE: *Ted and Mimi Gregg were among the World War II veterans who bought Fort William H. Seward from the Army and started the town of Port Chilkoot. They still live in their home on the fort, today a national historic site inside the town of Haines. (L.J. Campbell, staff)*

RIGHT: *Northern Southeast's Chilkat Tlingits gather in their traditional village of Klukwan, population about 130, along the Chilkat River. (Steve McCutcheon)*

Canal, one of Southeast's biggest salmon fisheries, supports the town, along with local government. Mining could figure in the future; developers of the Windy Craggy lead-

zinc mine in British Columbia propose shipping ore through town.

Haines Highway brings lots of visitors, many bound for the ferry. Residents often drive 250 miles to Whitehorse, Yukon Territory, for shopping and weekend vacations.

Haines hosts the Southeast Alaska State Fair each August, part of a farm legacy recalling pioneer Charlie Anway's famous giant strawberries. The fairgrounds holds the Dalton City movie set from "White Fang," filmed near Haines in 1990.

Native art and historical exhibits pack the Sheldon Museum downtown. The Gei-Sun Dancers, mostly Tlingit elders, and Chilkat Dancers perform regularly in summer.

Numerous Southeast carvers of note, including Nathan Jackson, started with Alaska Indian Arts, a carving workshop and gallery since 1957 located on historic Fort William Seward.

This 100-acre Army post of stately Neoclassical buildings operated 1904 to 1946. The following year, five veterans bought the property and made a renaissance town. The city later annexed the fort, today a national historical site. Every other year, the state community drama festival is held in the acclaimed Chilkat Center for the Arts on the fort.

Other communities in the area include settlements at Lutak and Mosquito Lake.

Skagway, on Lynn Canal's uppermost

finger, capitalizes today on its crazy gold rush history. The town of 700 caters to tourists, about 310,000 in 1992. Nearly half come by cruise ship. They stroll downtown boardwalks, shop in restored gold-rush-era buildings, ride horse-drawn buggies, and take in numerous attractions including the Klondike Gold Rush National Historical Park.

Skagway boomed overnight in the 1897 stampede to Canada's Klondike gold fields. Prospectors tramped over White Pass out of Skagway and Chilkoot Pass trail from Indian camp Dyea, three miles north. Today, Skagway is headquarters for backpackers tackling Chilkoot Pass trail, maintained by the National Park Service. For a time during the gold rush, notorious con man Soapy Smith ruled town, his doings among the theatrics carried on today for tourists.

The White Pass and Yukon Railway punched through the mountains in 1900 kept Skagway alive, carrying people and goods between tidewater and the interior until 1982. Today, trains offer summer passenger excursions. Klondike Highway 2 connects Skagway with the Alaska Highway. Along with tourism, Skagway depends on shipping. Canadian ore, when the mines are operating, and logs are trucked into town and go out on ships from Skagway's deep-water port.

BOTTOM LEFT: *Skagway's wild gold rush history propels a booming summer tourist trade at this community of 700 near the head of Lynn Canal. Klondike Highway 2 connects Skagway with the Alaska Highway, and the White Pass and Yukon Railway takes passengers to Lake Bennett along one of the traditional routes to the Klondike gold fields. (Harry M. Walker)*

BELOW: *The Haines Highway runs from Haines 150 miles north to Haines Junction on the Alaska Highway. Open year-round, the highway follows a gold rush pack trail blazed by pioneer Jack Dalton, and was upgraded during World War II to provide another route from tidewater to the Yukon. (Harry M. Walker)*

Glacier Bay: Echoes of the Ice Age

It's not so much the silence as the sound. The thunder of twitching ice pulses down the fiords, sweeping over a land just being born. This is Glacier Bay, a geographic landmark that didn't exist 200 years ago, and today is one of Southeast's main attractions.

About 50 miles west of Juneau, these convulsions shake the Fairweather forelands, where glacier movement and plant succession occur in a time frame easily grasped by passing humans. Capt. George Vancouver recorded no bay, only a shallow dent, when he sailed by in 1794; John Muir, 75 years later, wrote of rivers of ice calving bergs into ever-lengthening fiords. Botanists noted the pioneer plants colonizing gravel beds newly released by the ice, the shrubs and young trees growing where the ice had retreated decades earlier, and the climax forests of mature spruce and hemlock fringing the coast of Cross Sound and Icy Strait where the ice began its retreat.

Glacier Bay National Monument was formed in 1925 to protect this treasure; with 1980's Alaska National Interest Lands Conservation Act the region became Glacier Bay National Park and Preserve. Its 3.28 million acres are home to humpback and killer whales, mountain goats, bears, deer, porpoises and seals and myriad bird species. For years 30 to 40 humpbacks fed each summer in Glacier Bay. In 1992 this number dropped into the 20s, and National Park Service biologists are conducting a multiyear study to see if increased boat traffic is affecting the whales. In the meantime, concessionaires are offering boat trips to Point Adolphus, south across Icy Strait, to view humpbacks.

ABOVE: *Sumptuous meals of locally grown vegetables and locally caught seafood are a hallmark of Gustavus Inn. (Don Pitcher)*

TOP RIGHT: *Glacier Bay counts 13 active tidewater glaciers within its 65-mile length. Among those calving directly into the bay is Lamplugh in Johns Hopkins Inlet. Daily and overnight boat trips take visitors to the glaciers up the bay from park headquarters at Bartlett Cove. (Chip Porter)*

RIGHT: *The tiny community of Gustavus spreads along the shores of Icy Strait east of Glacier Bay. Access to the community is by scheduled air service or private plane, such as this Cessna 170B, or by scheduled boat or charter boat. (Harry M. Walker)*

LEFT: *Glacier Bay park is not all ice and saltwater. Its backcountry provides some spectacular vistas. This view shows the river running from Abyss Lake near Brady Glacier. (James R. Mackovjak)*

BELOW: *Among the more notorious of Alaska's landscapes is the haunting bay of Lituya, guarded by a dangerous bar, shaken by earth- quakes and scoured by deadly seismic sea waves. Many have died here and few have lingered. The forest edge on each side of the bay notes where a 1958 wave shaved the mountainsides. Cenotaph Island lies in the middle of the bay. (Chip Porter)*

Scheduled transport by plane or high-speed catamaran brings visitors to Gustavus, population 258, connected by a 10-mile road to park headquarters at Bartlett Cove. Gustavus' roots stem from home- steaders in the early 20th century who sought to grow fruits and vegetables for the market in Juneau and Hoonah.

Today residents look to fishing, government, seasonal work in the park, arts and crafts and subsis- tence to supply their needs. Gustavus' roads and lanes, mostly unpaved, spread out from the docks, past bed and breakfasts, noteworthy gardens, cabins lovingly crafted and decor- ated. Skiffs rest on the banks of the Salmon River, and the local fishing fleet goes after salmon and halibut.

The Alsek River borders the park on the north, a major rafting route drawing floaters worldwide. Proposed mining in the Alsek-Tatshenshinni drainage at Canada's Windy Craggy has disturbed park staff and rafters who consider industrial development unsuitable to the water quality of the Alsek and the pristine nature of the wilderness.

Within the park itself, commercial fishing in Glacier Bay and in Lituya Bay have sparked discussions on the appropriateness of commercial har- vests in a national park. Although legal in the preserve north and west of the park, commercial fishing is technically illegal in the park itself, but continues because as of early 1993 the ban was not enforced. A proposal to allow a 10-year exemp- tion nationwide for commercial fishing in national parks is under consideration.

■ Yakutat ■

Southeast's most remote arm extends north along a coastal plain from Glacier Bay National Park to Icy Bay. This plain largely consists of long, sandy beaches pounded relentlessly by ocean waves and backed by nearly impenetrable forests. The area includes the western slopes of the Saint Elias Mountains, Dry Bay, Yakutat Bay, the town of Yakutat, Russell Fiord Wilderness, Mount Saint Elias and several major glaciers — notably Malaspina, largest piedmont glacier in North America.

The Alsek River reaches the sea at Dry Bay, just north of Glacier Bay park boundary. The river drains 9,500 square miles in the United States and Canada through the mountains, its sediments nearly filling Dry Bay. The Alsek divides the Saint Elias Mountains to the north from the Fairweather Range, whose tallest peak, Mount Fairweather, reaches 15,300 feet.

North of Dry Bay, an outwash plain called Yakutat Forelands extends to Yakutat Bay. Western hemlock and Sitka spruce cover the forelands, the forest interspersed with clear-water streams popular with sport fishermen. The Situk River is famous for its steelhead trout. Above the forests, alpine tundra covers the highlands below the snow and ice of the Saint Elias.

Yakutat, northernmost community in Southeast, spreads along the shore of Monti Bay, an inlet on south Yakutat Bay. Earth-quakes in 1899 raised part of the shore of Yakutat Bay as much as 47 feet. The different heights of trees along the fault today reveal the uplift.

Yakutat Bay cuts into the east side of Malaspina Glacier and narrows into Disen-chantment Bay, where Hubbard Glacier meets seawater. Branching to the southeast, Russell Fiord cuts into Russell Fiord Wilderness.

Hubbard Glacier filled Yakutat Bay until about 600 years ago, when it began receding. In the past 100 years, it has advanced again, reducing Russell Fiord's entrance width to less than a mile. In 1986, the glacier closed off Russell Fiord for several months, trapping sea mammals and attracting worldwide attention. Experts think eventual closure is likely.

Yakutat, with about 740 people, half of Tlingit ancestry, depends on fishing. It is a center for steelhead and salmon sport fishing in Yakutat Forelands, where the U.S. Forest Service maintains cabins. A seafood processor buys salmon, halibut, black cod, herring, scallops and shrimp from the town's commercial fishermen.

The Native village corporation, Yak-Tat Kwaan, operates one of Southeast's larger oyster farms and is experimenting with scallop farming. Logging on Yak-Tat Kwaan lands near town provided jobs for about a decade until 1992, when most of the first-growth harvest ended.

Yakutat gets daily jet service to Anchorage, Juneau and other points. Cruise ships heading for Hubbard Glacier sometimes visit Yakutat.

On clear days from town, a panoramic view sweeps from 18,008-foot Mount Saint Elias on the north to Mount Fairweather on the south. Cannon Beach, a 15-mile-long

Large swatches of clear-cutting flank the forests around the fishing community of Yakutat, population 740, on Monti Bay. Larger Yakutat Bay is at left. (R.E. Johnson)

beachcombers' paradise, yields glass floats and other treasures. The beach's giant waves, 15- to 20-foot breakers, attract an international cadre of surfing fanatics. No locals partake, but surfers from as near as Sitka and as distant as Australia pilgrimage here, in T-shirts boasting "Yakutat Surfing Club." The surfers also wear insulating dry suits; summer water temperatures reach only about 40 degrees.

Tlingits occupied Yakutat when the Russians arrived in 1788. In 1795, the Russians established an agricultural colony, but in 1805, Yakutat Tlingits, angry at Russian meddling in their fishing, attacked and killed the 40 colonists. The Russians did not return. Smallpox in the late 1830s decimated the Tlingits; their population had doubled to 300 by the first American census in 1880. The community thrived in the 1920s with the

Yakutat & Southern Railroad hauling fish from Situk River to a salmon cannery in town.

North of Yakutat Bay, Malaspina Glacier — an 850-square-mile piedmont glacier almost the size of Rhode Island — engulfs the coastal plain. Rocks and soil mantle the glacier's edge, supporting large forests over stagnant ice. This ice occasionally shows in the walls of sinkholes, where trees collapse into melting ice. A lake on the southeast side of the glacier covers more than 20 square miles.

North of Malaspina Glacier, Icy Bay cuts northward to Guyot and Tyndall glaciers. Prior to 1904, Icy Bay did not exist because Guyot and Malaspina glaciers were connected. The glaciers retreated about 25 miles to form the bay, now popular with kayakers. Two decades of clear-cutting state forests along the coast west of Icy Bay ended in 1992.

TOP LEFT: *By early October 1986, Hubbard Glacier had advanced and blocked Russell Lake (right) from Disenchantment Bay, an offshoot of Yakutat Bay. On October 8, the ice dam broke, sending the water draining from the lake at about 3.7 million cubic feet per second. (R.E. Johnson)*

ABOVE: *Pacific Ocean surf pounds Cannon Beach, a favorite recreation site at Yakutat. Water weaves a sturdy lifeline for Southeasterners, who have found a home among the islands and mainland between the mountains and the sea. (R.E. Johnson)*

Art of Southeast Alaska's Natives

Wooden totem poles carved like ravens, eagles, beavers, bears, killer whales and an occasional human reach to the sky throughout Southeast. These monumental carvings are striking examples of the region's Native art and culture.

Southeast's Natives — Tlingits, Haidas and Tsimshians — are part of the Northwest Coast Indian culture, which included linguistically different groups from Yakutat to northern California. Theirs was a marine-based culture with elaborate social structures and rich ceremonial life, including dancing and gift-giving feasts called potlatches. From this came a distinctive art tradition.

Today, the art lives in community halls, cultural centers and homes. Traditional North-west Coast art includes wood carvings, spruce-root and cedar-bark baskets, bentwood boxes, carved silver, Chilkat and Raven's Tail weav-ings and dance regalia. Traditional designs also show up in non-traditional ways — in watercolors, pottery, wall murals, on T-shirts,

lapel pins, note cards and tourism brochures.

Northwest Coast art has evolved a highly refined style governed by formal principals of design and color. Briefly, black form lines establish shapes and design units. Form lines vary thin to thick and create illusions of motion. The most characteristic shape is the rounded rectangle, or ovoid. Animals representing clan crests are depicted in formalized abstractions to tell stories, relate family histories, or show wealth and position.

Southeast Natives excelled at wood carving. They built large timber houses, carving elaborate corner posts and screens, portable walls used by the chiefs for privacy. Some carvers specialized in making totems and canoes from massive cedar logs.

Totems could tell stories, hold the ashes of the dead, or ridicule. When completed, the pole-raising would become a village gala.

In 1939, the U.S. Forest Service salvaged old totems from abandoned villages and cemeteries throughout Southeast. They hired

Native carvers through the Civilian Conservation Corps to reproduce the most deteriorated; the reproductions today stand in places such as Totem Bight State Park in Ketchikan and parks in Saxman, Hydaburg and Klawock. The Totem Heritage Center in Ketchikan has many of the original old totems.

Indian carvers routinely made art of utilitarian items, etching intricate designs on wooden bowls and horn spoons. They made bentwood containers by kerfing, or cutting,

---

FACING PAGE: *Tlingit carver Nathan Jackson works on a totem at Saxman. Jackson began carving 25 years ago after a childhood spent watching carvers in the Haines and Juneau areas. He has created numerous totemic wood carvings on commission for public display and private collections. One of his larger works is the Eagle and Raven frieze around the* Juneau Empire *building on Juneau's waterfront. Jackson now lives in Ketchikan. (Don Pitcher)*

flat planks and shaping them with steam into square-cornered boxes.

Carving extended to silver. Carvers gained metal-working experience, making ceremonial pieces from copper obtained through trading. They hammered silver coins flat, carved them with traditional designs, and wore them as jewelry to display wealth. Contemporary artists today sometimes combine bentwood with basketry and silver carving.

Women traditionally twined baskets of spruce roots and cedar bark into a variety of shapes for carrying berries and fish. They also twined items such as hats, mats, fish nets and water buckets. They decorated baskets with contrasting plant materials, like maidenhair fern. A master basket maker today is Delores Churchill, a Haida in Ketchikan.

Baskets take hours of labor, including gathering and preparing materials. Spruce roots are dug, peeled, seasoned and separated into narrow threads. Tlingit weaver and basket maker Teri Rofkar, of Sitka, anticipates spring outings in the forest to strip cedar bark. A good pull yields a strip 50- to 60-feet long, and often involves climbing a steep slope alongside the tree. Sometimes she finds trees with scars made centuries ago by Indian women pulling bark for their baskets.

Closely related to basketry and carving is Chilkat and Raven's Tail blanket weaving. Dancers drape these robes over their shoulders, the blanket fringes swishing wildly in the dance. Chilkat blankets, which

The Sea Serpent and Bear-Up-The-Mountain totems stand outside the tribal house on Shakes Island in Wrangell harbor. These reproductions of old totems were carved during the U.S. Forest Service and Civilian Conservation Corps totem restoration project in the 1930s. (Steve McCutcheon)

originated with Tsimshians and were refined to their highest form by the Chilkat Tlingits, are made of mountain goat wool and cedar bark twined into totemic designs based on a painted pattern board. Ownership of a blanket was considered a sign of wealth, because of the hours required to make one. A blanket-making display with pattern board can be seen at the Sheldon Museum and Cultural Center in Haines.

Raven's Tail — blankets with geometric designs and tassels — predates Chilkat. Canadian weaver Cheryl Samuel resurrected the art after studying the few fragments of Raven's Tail robes in museums. Today, several Southeast weavers have learned Raven's Tail.

The Southeast Native dancing revival involves regalia making. Regalia includes

TOP RIGHT: *Chilkat Tlingit dancers perform in full regalia. (Steve McCutcheon)*

BOTTOM ROW: *Tlingit weaver Teri Rofkar (right) discusses her Raven's Tail robe at the Southeast Alaska Indian Cultural Center, Sitka. She has put in more than 250 hours to reach this halfway point. Her pattern, "Red Tide," commemorates Native sea otter hunters who died from eating poisoned mussels during Russian occupation.*

Raven's Tail, which early this century was called Tlingit northern geometric weaving, is characterized by bold linear black and white patterns and tassels. The five-sided Chilkat dancing blanket, shown far right, has curvilinear designs in the totemic genre. This Chilkat blanket is worn by a dancer in Haines.

Raven's Tail is woven in continuous horizontal rows left to right, from top to bottom. In Chilkat, no row between the heading and footing is continuous border to border; the designs are woven individually and interlocked. (Right, L.J. Campbell, staff; far right, John Warden)

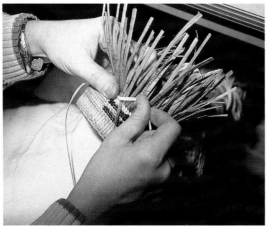

TOP LEFT: *This "Harnessing the Atom" totem, carved in 1967 by Tlingit Amos Wallace, stands amid English hawthorn flowers outside the Juneau-Douglas City Museum. With five figures — from top, Eagle, Russian Priest, Man, Sun and Raven — it symbolizes Raven creating the universe by releasing the Sun, Man harnessing energy of the universe, and the Russian and American influences on Southeast. The figure shown here is the Russian Priest with beard and folded arms. (Lynn Schooler)*

LEFT: *Northwest Coast Indian women excelled at basketry. Here, Tlingit weaver Teri Rofkar twines a yellow cedar-bark basket. Stems of maidenhair fern form the darker design. (L.J. Campbell, staff)*

ABOVE: *Carved wooden masks, such as this Tlingit bear mask of the Chilkat, represent another important expression of Northwest Coast talent. Masks traditionally were carved for ceremonial use to portray the relationahip of the tribe with spirits. (Steve McCutcheon)*

elaborate head dresses, carved masks and rattles, decorated pouches called octopus bags, and flannel dance robes with totemic crests outlined by buttons or abalone shells. Members of dance groups, like those in Kake, meet weekly with elders to make regalia. Dance groups perform throughout Southeast during summer. Dances and songs are private property and should not be taped without permission.

Many places in Southeast display Native art, in addition to those mentioned above:

■ **National Historical Park, Sitka:** Totems from the early 1900s, and contemporary artists working daily in the Southeast Alaska Indian Cultural Center, located at the park.

■ **Sheldon Jackson Museum, Sitka:** Collections from the 1800s, including Tlingit regalia, a dugout canoe and black argillite carvings unique to the Haida.

■ **Totem Heritage Center, Ketchikan:** Original old totems; extensive offering of Native art classes, including a certified two-year program of study.

■ **Chief Shakes Island, Wrangell:** The Tribal House of the Bear with replicas of four houseposts among the oldest in Alaska. Wrangell Museum houses the originals.

■ **Alaska State Museum, Juneau:** Permanent art collections and traveling displays of contemporary artists. Sealaska Corp. and the University of Alaska Southeast library, also in Juneau, have notable collections of contemporary work.

■ **Alaska Indian Arts, Haines:** Carvers at work; visitors welcome.

■ **Throughout Southeast:** Galleries and museum shops sell traditional Northwest Coast art and contemporary pieces with Northwest Coast influences.

Bibliography/Suggested Reading

Previous issues of *ALASKA GEOGRAPHIC*® have covered specific regions in Southeast in great detail. In addition, there are other publications that are noteworthy for their comprehensive coverage of the region's natural and man-made environment. Below is a list of earlier *ALASKA GEOGRAPHIC*® issues on Southeast, and our choices of comprehensive publications for those readers who want to explore the region in depth.

ALASKA GEOGRAPHIC® titles:

Admiralty Island, Fortress of the Bears, Vol. 18, No. 3, 1991

Alaska Native Arts and Crafts, Vol. 12, No. 3, 1985

Alaska's Forest Resources, Vol. 12, No. 2, 1985

Alaska's Glaciers, Vol. 9, No. 1, 1982, revised 1993

Alaska's Native People, Vol. 6, No. 3, 1979

Alaska's Weather, Vol. 18, No. 1, 1991

Glacier Bay, Icy Wilderness, Vol. 15, No. 1, 1988

Juneau, Vol. 17, No. 2, 1990

Sitka and Its Ocean/Island World, Vol. 9, No. 2, 1982

Skagway, A Legacy of Gold, Vol. 19, No. 1, 1992

The Chilkat River Valley, Vol. 11, No. 3, 1984

The Stikine River, Vol. 6, No. 4, 1979

Where Mountains Meet the Sea, Vol. 13, No. 1, 1986

Wrangell-Saint Elias, International Mountain Wilderness, Vol. 8, No. 1, 1981

■ ■ ■

Charles, Patricia, ed. *Spirit! Historic Ketchikan Alaska*. Ketchikan: Historic Ketchikan, Inc., 1992.

Drucker, Philip. *Cultures of the North Pacific Coast*. New York: Harper & Row Publishers Inc., 1965.

Emmons, George T. *The Tlingit Indians*. Frederica deLaguna, ed., Seattle, New York: University of Washington Press and American Museum of Natural History, 1991.

Eppenback, Sarah. *Alaska's Southeast, Touring the Inside Passage*. Chester, Conn.: The Globe Pequot Press, 1991.

Gunther, Erna. *Art in the Life of the Northwest Coast Indian*. Seattle: Superior Publishing Co., 1966.

Halpin, Marjorie M. *Totem Poles, An Illustrated Guide*. Seattle: University of Washington Press, 1981.

Holm, Bill. *Northwest Coast Indian Art: An Analysis of Form*. Seattle: University of Washington Press, 1965.

Muir, John. *Travels in Alaska*. With Foreword by John Haines. San Francisco: Sierra Club Books, 1988.

O'Clair, Rita M., Robert H. Armstrong, Richard Carstensen. *The Nature of Southeast Alaska*. Bothell, Wash.: Alaska Northwest Books, 1992.

Paul, Frances. *Spruce Root Basketry of the Alaska Tlingit*. Lawrence, Kan.: U.S. Dept. of Interior, Bureau of Indian Affairs, 1944, with appendix by Nora Florendo Dauenhauer, 1981.

Piggott, Margaret. *Discover Southeast Alaska with Pack & Paddle*. Seattle: The Mountaineers, 1990.

Stewart, Hilary. *Cedar*. Seattle: University of Washington Press, 1984.

Index

ALASKA GEOGRAPHIC® back issues

The North Slope, Vol. 1, No. 1. Charter issue. Out of print.

One Man's Wilderness, Vol. 1, No. 2. Out of print.

Admiralty...Island in Contention, Vol. 1, No. 3. $7.50.

Fisheries of the North Pacific, Vol. 1, No. 4. Out of print.

Alaska-Yukon Wild Flowers Guide, Vol. 2, No. 1. Out of print.

Richard Harrington's Yukon, Vol. 2, No. 2. Out of print.

Prince William Sound, Vol. 2, No. 3. Out of print.

Yakutat: The Turbulent Crescent, Vol. 2, No. 4. Out of print.

Glacier Bay: Old Ice, New Land, Vol. 3, No. 1. Out of print.

The Land: Eye of the Storm, Vol. 3, No. 2. Out of print.

Richard Harrington's Antarctic, Vol. 3, No. 3. $12.95.

The Silver Years, Vol. 3, No. 4. $17.95.

Alaska's Volcanoes: Northern Link In the Ring of Fire, Vol. 4, No. 1. Out of print.

The Brooks Range, Vol. 4, No. 2. Out of print.

Kodiak: Island of Change, Vol. 4, No. 3. Out of print.

Wilderness Proposals, Vol. 4, No. 4. Out of print.

Cook Inlet Country, Vol. 5, No. 1. Out of print.

Southeast: Alaska's Panhandle, Vol. 5, No. 2. Out of print.

Bristol Bay Basin, Vol. 5, No. 3. Out of print.

Alaska Whales and Whaling, Vol. 5, No. 4. $19.95.

Yukon-Kuskokwim Delta, Vol. 6, No. 1. Out of print.

Aurora Borealis, Vol. 6, No. 2. $14.95.

Alaska's Native People, Vol. 6, No. 3. $24.95.

The Stikine River, Vol. 6, No. 4. $12.95.

Alaska's Great Interior, Vol. 7, No. 1. $17.95.

Photographic Geography of Alaska, Vol. 7, No. 2. Out of print.

The Aleutians, Vol. 7, No. 3. $19.95.

Klondike Lost, Vol. 7, No. 4. Out of print.

Wrangell-Saint Elias, Vol. 8, No. 1. $19.95.

Alaska Mammals, Vol. 8, No. 2. $15.95.

The Kotzebue Basin, Vol. 8, No. 3. $15.95.

Alaska National Interest Lands, Vol. 8, No. 4. $17.95.

Alaska's Glaciers, Vol. 9, No. 1. Revised 1993. $19.95.

Sitka and Its Ocean/Island World, Vol. 9, No. 2. $19.95.

Islands of the Seals: The Pribilofs, Vol. 9, No. 3. $12.95.

Alaska's Oil/Gas & Minerals Industry, Vol. 9, No. 4. $15.95.

Adventure Roads North, Vol. 10, No. 1. $17.95.

Anchorage and the Cook Inlet Basin, Vol. 10, No. 2. $17.95.

Alaska's Salmon Fisheries, Vol. 10, No. 3. $15.95.

Up the Koyukuk, Vol. 10, No. 4. $17.95.

Nome: City of the Golden Beaches, Vol. 11, No. 1. $14.95.

Alaska's Farms and Gardens, Vol. 11, No. 2. $15.95.

Chilkat River Valley, Vol. 11, No. 3. $15.95.

Alaska Steam, Vol. 11, No. 4. $14.95.

Northwest Territories, Vol. 12, No. 1. $17.95.

Alaska's Forest Resources, Vol. 12, No. 2. $16.95.

Alaska Native Arts and Crafts, Vol. 12, No. 3. $17.95.

Our Arctic Year, Vol. 12, No. 4. $15.95.

Where Mountains Meet the Sea: Alaska's Gulf Coast, Vol. 13, No. 1. $17.95.

Backcountry Alaska, Vol. 13, No. 2. $17.95.

British Columbia's Coast, Vol. 13, No. 3. $17.95.

Lake Clark/Lake Iliamna Country, Vol. 13, No. 4. Out of print.

Dogs of the North, Vol. 14, No. 1. $17.95.

South/Southeast Alaska, Vol. 14, No. 2. Out of print.

Alaska's Seward Peninsula, Vol. 14, No. 3. $15.95.

The Upper Yukon Basin, Vol. 14, No. 4. $17.95.

Glacier Bay: Icy Wilderness, Vol. 15, No. 1. Out of print.

Dawson City, Vol. 15, No. 2. $15.95.

Denali, Vol. 15, No. 3. $16.95.

The Kuskokwim River, Vol. 15, No. 4. $17.95.

Katmai Country, Vol. 16, No. 1. $17.95.

North Slope Now, Vol. 16, No. 2. $14.95.

The Tanana Basin, Vol. 16, No. 3. $17.95.

The Copper Trail, Vol. 16, No. 4. $17.95.

The Nushagak Basin, Vol. 17, No. 1. $17.95.

Juneau, Vol. 17, No. 2. $17.95.

The Middle Yukon River, Vol. 17, No. 3. $17.95.

The Lower Yukon River, Vol. 17, No. 4. $17.95.

Alaska's Weather, Vol. 18, No. 1. $17.95.

Alaska's Volcanoes, Vol. 18, No. 2. $17.95.

Admiralty Island: Fortress of the Bears, Vol. 18, No. 3. $17.95.

Unalaska/Dutch Harbor, Vol. 18, No. 4. $17.95.

Skagway: A Legacy of Gold, Vol. 19, No. 1. $18.95.

ALASKA: The Great Land, Vol. 19, No. 2. $18.95.

Kodiak, Vol. 19, No. 3. $18.95.

Alaska's Railroads, Vol. 19, No. 4. $18.95.

Prince William Sound, Vol. 20, No. 1. $18.95.

ALL PRICES SUBJECT TO CHANGE

Your $39 membership in The Alaska Geographic Society includes four subsequent issues of *ALASKA GEOGRAPHIC*®, the Society's official quarterly. Please add $10 for non-U.S. memberships.

Additional membership information is available on request. Single copies of the *ALASKA GEOGRAPHIC*® back issues are also available. When ordering, please make payments in U.S. funds and add $2.00 postage/handling per copy book rate; $4.00 per copy for Priority Mail. Non-U.S. postage extra. Free catalog available. To order back issues send your check or money order and volumes desired to:

The Alaska Geographic Society

**P.O. Box 93370
Anchorage, AK 99509**

NEXT ISSUE: *Arctic National Wildlife Refuge*, Vol. 20, No. 2. In Alaska's northeastern corner sits a wonderland known as ANWR. One of the state's last true wildernesses, ANWR is the subject of intense interest from oil companies that seek to explore under its coastal plain. This issue details the region's natural resources, human use of those resources for subsistence and the politics that make ANWR such a controversial corner. To members 1993, with index. $18.95.

THE NEWSLETTER
ALASKA GEOGRAPHIC®

Steve McCutcheon, among
Anchorage's earliest
residents...see page 117

Alaska's Wolves

By Bill Sherwonit

EDITOR'S NOTE: *Bill, a freelance writer, has contributed several articles to* ALASKA GEOGRAPHIC®, *including substantial sections of* Dogs of the North, *Vol. 14, No. 1, and* Up The Koyukuk, *Vol. 10, No. 4. Bill is also the author of the book* Iditarod, The Great Race to Nome.

After a two-year lull, Alaska's long-running and often heated debate about wolf-management practices re-ignited in fall 1992 when the state Board of Game announced plans to resurrect a controversial predator control program last implemented in the mid-1980s.

Those plans sparked a nationwide protest that threatened Alaska's tourism industry and eventually prompted state officials to indefinitely suspend any wolf-control programs.

Above all, perhaps, this latest round of acrimonious debate demonstrated that Alaska's wildlife managers can no longer ignore national attitudes toward *Canis lupus* — attitudes that currently favor wolf preservation rather than wolf control by an overwhelming margin — when formulating future management policies.

In mid-November 1992, the Game Board approved a proposal by the Alaska Department of Fish

A female wolf patrols the Sable Pass area of Denali National Park. Females give birth to litters of from four to seven pups in May or June; by early winter they grow to nearly adult size, 100 pounds for males, 10 to 15 pounds lighter for females. *(Steve McCutcheon)*

and Game's Division of Wildlife Conservation to kill wolves to boost caribou and moose populations in Alaska's Interior.

The reduction program called for state-employed biologists, working from helicopters, to shoot as many as 330 wolves during a three- to five-year period to increase caribou and moose populations in areas of the state where the goal is to manage those prey species for priority use by humans. The proposal called for up to an

additional 70 wolves to be killed by land-based measures. Whenever possible, entire packs would be eliminated in what one state biologist described as a "surgical" operation. In some instances the animals would be tracked using radio-collars ostensibly placed on the wolves for research purposes.

In the judgment of the Game Board, the department and wolf-control advocates, such drastic actions were necessary to prevent moose and caribou numbers from

collapsing into what biologists call a "predator pit," from which they may take decades to recover. "The object is to knock (wolf) numbers down in a hurry," said department spokesman Bruce Bartley. "In the long run, both prey and wolves will benefit."

Control opponents, including some wolf biologists outside the department, criticized the plan. Support for the plan was not unanimous within the department, but the proposal was thought to be the best compromise, according to Cathie Harms, a department biologist who worked on the planning process.

State officials anticipated some public outcry, but the backlash that followed exceeded all expectations. Thousands of people from across the nation wrote letters of protest to Gov. Walter Hickel, as well as to the Division of Wildlife Conservation. Animal-rights groups initiated high-profile boycotts against Alaska's tourism industry and staged demonstrations in several of the country's largest cities. An Oregon congressman vowed to introduce legislation that would prohibit state-sanctioned aerial hunts.

In early December, responding to pressure from within and outside the state, Gov. Hickel suspended the proposal until a mid-January Alaska Wolf Summit in Fairbanks could be held. Major players in the debate — biologists, conservationists, hunters, trappers, animal-rights activists and state wildlife managers — would meet to consider "fresh and workable approaches to wolf and wildlife management."

A few weeks later, department Commissioner Carl Rozier announced that department personnel would not conduct aerial control of wolves, at least through 1993.

More than 100 participants, including many from the Lower 48, were invited to the summit. Although they reached consensus on certain issues, the various interest groups were, as expected, unable to resolve the primary issue of wolf control.

Following the summit, Board of Game members unanimously, but reluctantly, voted to cancel the wolf-control program it had approved in November. The board also directed the Department of Fish and Game to revise its statewide Strategic Wolf Management Plan, which had been completed only a year earlier.

Both the aborted wolf-control

This wolf listens for the chattering of ground squirrels in the Alaska Range. (Steve McCutcheon)

program and the department's wolf-management plan had their roots in a citizens' planning team, born in 1990 during Gov. Steve Cowper's administration.

Ironically, that 12-member team, a disparate group representing virtually the full spectrum of human attitudes toward wolves, was supposed to find some "middle ground" in Alaska's long-running wolf debate and help Fish and Game develop management strategies acceptable to all of the state's interest groups.

"The main purpose of creating the citizen planning team was to end the controversy," says Stephen Wells, associate director of the Alaska Wildlife Alliance and staunch wolf-control opponent.

"But the department subverted that public process to meet its own agenda. And in so doing, it started a firestorm of epic proportions."

Dick Bishop, wolf-control advocate and former regional supervisor for the department in Fairbanks, counters: "The consumptive use of wildlife for food and other values . . . is paramount in many Alaskan's lives. In much of the state because of federal laws and ecological limitations, intensive management is impossible. The Board of Game and the department in proposing and authorizing intensive management of predators and prey on 3 percent of Alaska's lands made a biologically sound and socially responsible decision to

accommodate those consumptive use values, recognizing that nonconsumptive values were broadly accommodated on federal lands and on the additional 3 percent of state lands on which the board gave complete protection to wolves. The board and the department did not subvert the intent of the wolf planning team or of the broad public interest in sound conservation and management of predator/prey systems in Alaska. They did not . . . threaten the viability of wolf populations in areas authorized for intensive management or in the state as a whole...."

It remains to be seen whether the citizen group's effort to find some middle ground will prove fruitful. But clearly Alaska's on-going wolf debate is far from ended.

It's also clear that public perceptions of the wolf have changed dramatically since Alaska's territorial days. Then wolves were primarily treated as undesirable vermin that competed with humans for food and therefore needed to be controlled, if not eliminated. Beginning with statehood in 1959, some attitudes and policies reflected an effort to conserve wolves. Nowadays, a large and steadily growing number of people view the wolf as a symbol of the wilderness, an animal to be protected, not destroyed.

While wolves have been removed from most of their former range in the Lower 48, they occupy nearly their entire historic range in Alaska, and are common throughout 85 percent of the state from Southeast to the North Slope.

Fish and Game's most recent estimate of Alaska's wolf population is 6,000 to 7,000 animals, spread among some 700 to 900 packs. Wolf numbers are stable or increasing throughout the state, with population densities ranging from one wolf per 25 to 75 square miles in Southeast to one wolf per 150 square miles in northern and western Alaska.

Highly social animals, wolves usually live in family units called packs. Most number six to 12 animals, but some packs with up to 30 or 40 members have been reported. Most packs have home ranges, or territories, that they defend from other wolves. Territories are marked by scent posts (sites where wolves have urinated on objects such as rocks or trees) and vary from 200 to 800 square miles. Range size depends on a variety of factors such as availability of food, pack size, terrain, weather and the presence of competing packs.

The pack is characterized by an elaborate hierarchy, with the highest-ranking male and female being designated the "alpha pair." That hierarchy is maintained largely through ritualistic behavior; except in times of extreme stress, fighting within packs is uncommon.

"Wolves are at the pinnacle of social development," Gordon Haber, an independent wolf researcher, says. "Pups have a prolonged educational dependency on adults and packs use extraordinary forms of cooperation to feed on physically superior prey."

Wolves vary in color, ranging from black to almost white; those in Southeast tend to be darker than those found in the rest of Alaska. *(Steve McCutcheon)*

Breeding, preceded by a lengthy courtship, usually occurs in February or March, with litters of four to seven pups (five is the average) born in May or June. As a rule, packs have one litter per year, but in some instances two or three females in a single pack may produce litters.

Pups remain in their dens, which typically are dug into well-drained, south-facing slopes, for about three weeks, the period they're most susceptible to predation by bears, eagles or even ravens. Their mother may leave the den for a short time; when she does, another adult acts as baby-sitter. Other pack members bring food, usually carried in their stomachs and later regurgitated, from successful hunts to the den.

Weaning is completed by midsummer and the den is exchanged for a series of rendez-vous sites. Pups weigh 30 to 40 pounds by September. By early winter and now approaching adult size — adult males average about 100 pounds; females are 10 to 15 pounds lighter — they are capable of traveling and hunting with the pack, which abandons its rendezvous sites and begins its seasonal nomadic lifestyle.

Though known officially as the gray wolf, Alaska's subspecies of *Canis lupus* exhibit a wide range of colors. About 70 percent are various shades of gray, often mixed with tans or browns, while 25 percent are black and 1 to 2 percent are white. Wolves in Southeast, generally considered to be a different subspecies, tend to be darker than those in the state's northern reaches.

Alaska's wolves depend mainly on large hoofed mammals for their survival. Moose and caribou are their principal prey throughout most of the state, but Dall sheep, Sitka black-tailed deer and mountain goats are important in some regions. Other food sources include snowshoe hares, beavers, lemmings, voles, ground squirrels and occasionally birds or fish.

Based on extensive studies, biologists have determined that wolves that depend mainly on moose make kills every three to eight days; those relying primarily on caribou or sheep kill prey every one to three days. In times of scarcity, however, wolves can survive without food for weeks.

Because wolves are opportunistic feeders, they prey most heavily on young, old, injured or diseased animals. Battles with healthy, mature prey are generally not worth the risk of injury or death, though in some circumstances wolves are capable of killing animals in their prime.

Hunts are led by the alpha animal; the rest of the pack usually strings out single file. Techniques vary considerably and may include stalking, ambush or relay hunting. One common method is to catch prey by surprise and cut off avenues of escape.

Wolves are good swimmers and have been known to attack prey in the water. This wolf swims the Yukon River. *(Steve McCutcheon)*

The neck and hindquarters are preferred targets when an attack ensues. Once a kill is made, wolves will gorge themselves with meat. Six to eight animals can consume an entire caribou in just a few hours. According to Harms, who is familiar with Fish and Game prey consumption rate studies, six to eight wolves can consume an entire young Dall sheep in under an hour.

Normally wolves kill and consume one prey animal at a time. Occasionally, however, they engage in what scientists call "surplus killing."

"At certain times, wolves do kill more than they eat," says wildlife scientist Vic Van Ballenberghe. "It's dramatic when it happens, but it's rare. Normally wolves have difficulty killing enough to eat. They're not some kind of vacuum cleaner sucking up animals at will."

Humans are the major source of wolf mortality in Alaska. During the last decade about 1,000 wolves have been killed annually by hunters and trappers, but the availability of habitat and prey, rather than human harvest, is considered a more important factor in limiting wolf numbers.

Another significant factor is other wolves. State biologist Bob Stephenson has estimated that, in some regions of Alaska, from 10 to 20 percent of all wolf mortalities are caused by other wolves. With

few exceptions, victims are usually wolves that have been caught trespassing in another pack's territory.

Other causes of death include disease, injuries, predation on small pups by eagles or bears, incapacitation caused by porcupine quills and starvation. Few wolves live beyond five years, though some may survive to 14 or 15.

Because encounters with other packs may lead to injury or even death, wolves frequently announce their whereabouts by howling.

"Howling enables wolves to communicate their presence over distances of several miles," Stephenson says. "It keeps adjacent packs aware of each other."

Biologists have noted that wolves howl most readily at kills

and when they are around pups. They also howl to locate other pack members, signal alarm, release anxiety and sometimes, perhaps, to playfully join in a group sing-along.

When they howl together, wolves harmonize by choosing different keys. Two or three wolves singing together may sound like a chorus of a dozen or more.

Although most wolves travel in packs, an unknown number spend at least part of their lives as loners. Biologists say it's not unusual for yearlings, or old wolves, to disperse from family groups and travel long distances in apparently random directions. One radio-collared wolf, for example, traveled from the Kenai Peninsula to the Fairbanks area, a distance of

several hundred miles. Another moved from the Nelchina Basin to the Brooks Range, more than 400 miles away.

Stephenson describes lone wolves as the "invisible part" of Alaska's wolf population and estimates they may number as many as 1,000 to 2,000 animals. Many loners eventually join a new pack, or find a mate and form their own family group.

Dispersal behavior helps explain why wolves throughout Alaska have such similar characteristics and why they can so quickly recolonize regions where the wolf population has been decimated. "It's remarkable how quickly they fill the gap," Stephenson says. "If there's a vacuum it won't last long, if suitable habitat is available. There's a constant movement, as new wolves come into a region and others move out."

Despite renewed debate about management strategies and priorities, evidence suggests that Alaska's wolf population continues to thrive. The biggest threat to their long-term well-being is not harvest by trappers and hunters but dramatic increases in the state's human population, development, habitat degradation and reduced prey numbers.

As the citizen planning team noted in its final report to the Department of Fish and Game, "Alaska is fortunate to have one of the larger wolf populations in the world and currently has extensive habitat and prey. Therefore, we (Alaskans) have a special responsibility to ensure that wolves and their habitat are conserved."

Steve McCutcheon, Alaskan

By Charles P. Wohlforth

EDITOR'S NOTE: *Charles is a free-lance writer living in Anchorage and a former* Anchorage Daily News *reporter.*

In the rows of photographic filing cabinets in Steve McCutcheon's basement reside the 70,000 keys to his memory. And living in his memory is the entire span of Anchorage history.

McCutcheon's photograph collection is an Alaska pioneer's vision of what matters. Photographs, by the tens of thousands, not of people, but of things. Mostly useful ones. There are images of geology, wildlife, the sea, and a whole room of pictures of the building of the trans-Alaska pipeline.

And every image is useful in itself. McCutcheon, at 81, says he never worried about putting his work in art galleries because you can't make money that way. But he makes a good annual living selling stock pictures he has taken during the last 50 years to publishers of

Lifelong Alaskan Steve McCutcheon photographs the Grand Canyon of the Stikine River near Telegraph Creek, British Columbia, east of Wrangell, in May 1991. *(Courtesy of Steve McCutcheon)*

textbooks, magazines, makers of films and advertisers.

When McCutcheon receives a request for an image — a glacier he shot on a trip 30 years ago, an oil tanker, an ice crystal — he is almost never stumped. Everything is here in these cabinets.

His filing system?

McCutcheon simply points to his head.

"The catalogue's up here," he says. "I have a very poor memory, but that's one thing I can remember. When I look at a picture, I can remember where and when."

That covers a lot of where and when. Steve McCutcheon, tall and physically impressive to this day, came to Anchorage as a small boy when the city was just a tent camp on the banks of Ship Creek. He believes he is the city's earliest living resident.

Stephen Douglas McCutcheon was born in Cordova, August 30, 1911. His father was railroadman, entrepreneur and successful Nome gold-seeker Herbert Hazard McCutcheon; his mother, Clara Krueger McCutcheon, had come north to feed the crews building the Copper River & Northwestern Railroad before she became Chitina's first bride.

Many years later, Steve McCutcheon met the "doctor" who delivered him.

"You Bert McCutcheon's boy?" the doctor asked him. "You have a singular distinction. You were my first cash baby. I'd been dealing mostly in duck and geese and chickens, but when you were born, your dad came in and gave me a crisp new $50 bill."

"I've since learned he wasn't really a medical man. He was a veterinarian," McCutcheon says.

The family moved to Anchorage for the building of the Alaska Railroad in September 1915. H. H. McCutcheon bought a lot in the original town site auction. After a cold winter living in a tent, he built a house for his family out of the logs cut from his land on Seventh Avenue. There his wandering days ended — Steve McCutcheon's father lived in that house, or next door, the rest of his life. His mother remained in the house on Seventh until before the 1964 earthquake, when she moved to a house on 11th. She eventually entered the Anchorage Pioneers Home where she was living when she died in 1986.

H. H. McCutcheon was foreman of the Anchorage railroad yards

TOP LEFT: Born in Cordova in August 1911, Steve McCutcheon moved with his parents, H.H. McCutcheon and Clara Krueger McCutcheon, to Anchorage in 1915. This 1918 photo shows the Anchorage Public School on the south side of Fifth Avenue between F and G streets. Elementary classes were held on the lower two floors, high school classes on the top floor. Seven-year-old Steve, looking down and wearing a light-colored necktie, is the fifth child from right in the next to back row. *(Courtesy of Steve McCutcheon)*

ABOVE: Steve McCutcheon, third from left in back row, joins his teammates on the first string of the Anchorage High School basketball team of 1930. With Steve in front row are: Odin Strandberg, Lawrence Bayer and Ted Strandberg; in back are Coach Thompson, Bob Knapp, Peter Shadura and Bob Carlson. *(Courtesy of Steve McCutcheon)*

and a member of the city council. With Oscar Gill he chose the site of Merrill Field. In 1931, he was elected to the territorial legislature.

Steve McCutcheon began working for the railroad in 1928, at age 17, and worked his way up through a variety of jobs to become foreman of a power station in Curry at age 24. That was where he became a photographer.

"There was no place to go and not much to do except mush around the hills," he says. For a hobby he chose between shooting pictures and shooting game; for the next 50 years of his travels throughout the state and much of the world, he took pictures of everything he saw.

"When I'm out I shoot everything that's going by. Everything," he says. "To be a good photographer of this type of thing, you have to know about... a lot of things."

McCutcheon's various careers and frontier self-reliance gave him some of that knowledge. The rest he got from books on the natural sciences he still studies to identify plants and geological formations.

With no higher to go in the railroad, he quit in 1940 and became a deputy U.S. marshal, using his youth and size to intimidate drunks and criminals in towns and villages from Talkeetna to Dillingham. A year later he became deputy commissioner of labor for the territory. And a year after that he was hired as the manager of the wartime Office of Price Administration for the entire northern half of the state. In that job he trekked from a base in

Fairbanks across the territory by dog sled, river boat and airplane to establish price controls in tiny village stores. Again, his size and longevity in Alaska helped.

BELOW: Drafted for military service in 1944, Steve spent the next couple of years in the Army, until his father's death in 1945 created a vacancy in the territorial Senate. He was elected to fill his father's unexpired term, and remained in the territorial legislature until 1953. *(Courtesy of Steve McCutcheon)*

RIGHT: After working his way up as far as he could go in the Alaska Railroad, he quit in 1940 and became a deputy U.S. marshal. By 1943 he was manager of the wartime Office of Price Administration for the northern half of the territory. From his headquarters in Fairbanks, where this photo was taken, he traveled widely, convincing Alaskans to go along with the government's program. *(Courtesy of Steve McCutcheon)*

FOR TERRITORIAL
SENATOR
VOTE FOR
Sgt. STEVE McCUTCHEON
To Fill the Unexpired Term of the Late Senator H. H. McCutcheon
Special Election - January 29, 1946

"There was a lot of kicking and screaming," he says. "A lot of these guys were up in Alaska because they were at the end of the road, they didn't want government

interference, and they wanted to do things their way. About the way the guys are up in Fairbanks now."

In 1944, McCutcheon was drafted, but within two years was

FAIRBANKS 1943

running for the territorial legislature.

"Every sergeant on the base put a sign in his window," he says.

His father had served 14 years in the office, including as Speaker of the House, until dying in 1945. Steve was elected to replace him, received a special Army discharge and stayed in the legislature until 1953. His late brother, Stanley, also spent many of those years in the legislature. At the territory's constitutional convention in Fairbanks in 1955, Steve served as one of the at-large delegates and chaired the committee on the judiciary.

And he photographed everything that happened. "I've got total coverage," he says.

In 1946, McCutcheon had used a loan from a veterans fund created by the territorial legislature to open Mac's Photo Shop on Anchorage's Fourth Avenue. He sold cameras, processed film and took pictures of everything he saw.

During those years, McCutcheon knew history was passing, and he documented the changes around him.

"People didn't expect Anchorage to become a city," he says. "Up until the military came in the '40s, the bulk of the thought was to build quickly, for temporary use, make your money, and then get out."

That attitude only changed with the discovery of oil on the Kenai Peninsula in the 1950s, McCutcheon says.

"I think that was the first time anyone thought that Anchorage might actually be a place that would stay here," he says. "If we hadn't gotten oil, Anchorage wouldn't be one tenth the size it is now."

McCutcheon had enough faith in the city's future to document its growth at a time when few were thinking about history. Each year he took an aerial photograph of

BOTTOM LEFT: After World War II, Steve opened Mac's Photo, shown here in 1947, on Fourth Avenue in downtown Anchorage. The 1964 earthquake destroyed the building, and Mac's Photo moved to Steve's former home on Seventh Avenue. *(Courtesy of Steve McCutcheon)*

BELOW: Steve took up photography as his profession in 1935. He is shown here photographing scenes in the Chugach Mountains east of Anchorage in August 1952. *(Courtesy of Steve McCutcheon)*

RIGHT: In 1960 Steve visited the Pribilof Islands in the Bering Sea to tape vocalizations of a northern fur seal pup. *(Courtesy of Steve McCutcheon)*

the growing city. Together, those photographs show a town that at first barely reached Chester Creek to the south but later expanded to fill the Anchorage bowl. His own house, which he shares with his wife, Gloria, sits on the south shore of Campbell Lake. It was all by itself out in the country when it was built. Now, outside his picture windows, housing crowds the lake.

But McCutcheon says he is pleased with the changes.

"I think Alaska has gone ahead. There's only two ways to go. Ahead or behind. I think it's for the better. It's a lot more comfortable living here, now that you don't have to pack your water and go out the back door to the biffy."

When his store was destroyed in the 1964 earthquake, McCutcheon took photographs of that, too. The book of earthquake photographs he published later helped him recoup the cost of $40,000 worth of cameras that were buried in the hole into which his shop fell.

"There was a lot of reconstruction," he says. "There was a lot of work. I got an awful lot of work shooting structures either to demonstrate damage or no damage. It was probably a boom in disguise of a catastrophe."

BELOW: This shingled bungalow is the original home that H.H. McCutcheon built in summer 1916. In this 1962 photo, Clara Krueger McCutcheon, Steve's mother, surveys the garden she kept for many years at 310 West Seventh Ave. *(Courtesy of Steve McCutcheon)*

RIGHT: In 1964, Carl Brady, then president of the Anchorage Chamber of Commerce, presents Steve McCutcheon with the chamber's first Gold Pan Award given to an individual. *(Courtesy of Steve McCutcheon)*

One set of photographs from that book demonstrates McCutcheon's documentary vision of the world. A six story tall, concrete apartment building just had been erected in downtown Anchorage using a new method of construction. Thinking the contrast of the building's modernity with a log cabin that stood in front of it might make a salable picture, McCutcheon shot the image shortly before the quake. After the earthquake, he shot the same picture from the same angle. Only this time, the cabin was all that showed up in the frame — the apartment building had disappeared, falling flat to the ground.

His files of stock pictures already were so extensive by that time that in his book McCutcheon was able to include several before-and-after comparisons — of the peeled-open J.C. Penney's department store, the collapsed Government Hill Elementary School and the fractured Turnagain neighborhood as seen from the air.

Those photographs, like all of McCutcheon's photography, show a sharp clarity of composition and intention. His photographic impulse was always documentary — the picture is used to show its subject as accurately and precisely as possible, without the photographer's ideas getting into the way. Contrast and lighting are usually sharp, contrasting textures

are highlighted and depth of field is broadened to create a world in which everything is in sharp focus.

When he talks about the rewards of his work, McCutcheon first mentions the satisfaction of doing a good job that is useful to the client, not a creative or artistic vision.

"Maybe you had to have a more practical view, because you had to scramble to put a few beans on the table," he says. "Young people today seem to have had it a lot easier, and they have the luxury of spending time thinking about who they are and what they want to do."

But McCutcheon's view of Alaska is permanently recorded in Alaska history, most strongly in the well-known photographs he took of the building of the trans-Alaska pipeline. In 1970, McCutcheon decided he wanted the assignment and bought a truck to drive north over the pipeline haul road, now called the Dalton Highway. On returning to Anchorage, he showed his photographs to Alyeska Pipeline Service Co. executives, who named him the pipeline's official photographer. During the next eight years, he would shoot more than 30,000 images of the pipeline. Many of those pictures became famous, such as a shot of two welders' torches about to meet finishing the line's final weld.

But it is the lesser shots that fill his cabinets that make up the real photographic legacy of Steve McCutcheon. He recorded not only the big events in Alaska history, but the everyday images that make up real life experience.

Recently, McCutcheon gave 49,872 of his most historic black-and-white images to the Anchorage Museum of History and Art, including some photographs he received from the painter Sydney Laurence.

"I intend, when the last bell rings, that it'll all go to the museum," he says.

But not the catalogue. That's his to keep.

LEFT: Steve (right) and brother Stanley discuss the finer points of fishing during an outing on a tributary creek of the Skwentna River in the late 1960s. *(Courtesy of Steve McCutcheon)*

BELOW: In March 1970, Steve drove the haul road, then known as the Hickel Highway and now called the Dalton Highway, carefully documenting his trip for a later pitch to Alyeska Pipeline Service Co. officials. The executives liked what they saw, and signed a multi-year contract with Steve naming him the consortium's official photographer. *(Courtesy of Steve McCutcheon)*

S H A R I N G

THEY PUT OLD HARBOR ON THE MAP

I really appreciate your sending me the Kodiak edition — it's wonderful. We were in seafood processing many years. In fact, my husband pioneered Dungeness crab in Ketchikan.

We like to think we put Old Harbor on the map. We used to have the *Sonya* that was anchored there. We also had the *Skookum Chief* in Kodiak and the *Aleutian Fjord* that went mostly to Dutch Harbor. Also the *Pacific Pearl*, now known as *Alaska Fresh Seafood*. Dave Woodruff [vice president and manager of Alaska operations for Alaska Fresh Seafood, Inc.] used to work for us.

—*Mary Furfiord*
Seattle, Washington

MAIL BOAT PHOTOS, ANYONE?

The recent issue on Kodiak brought back many pleasurable memories, namely the one- to two-day layovers our family had in Kodiak while traveling on the old mail boat run from Seward to Nikolski back in the 1950s. For many years up until the 1960s, the bulk of the mail service to the villages from Chignik to Nikolski was provided on a monthly basis via a mail boat run originating and ending in Seward. Our family first came to Alaska in 1957. In September we flew from Seattle to Anchorage to Kodiak where we boarded the M.V. *Expansion.* We were headed to Perryville with some friends who were teachers there. A couple of months later we again caught the *Expansion* on its out-bound run west to Pavloff Harbor on Sanak Island where my parents taught for two years. Living on an isolated island like Sanak, which had a population of 50 to 60, made the monthly appearance of the *Expansion* with its mail, freight and fresh foods such as fruits and vegetables an important event. The same also held true for many other villages such as Perryville, Belkofski, False Pass, Akutan and Nikolski, among others.

In those days everyone was more isolated and air service was limited. In fact, Reeves only started once a week service between Cold Bay and Sand Point in 1957. Without the mail boat, some of the villages such as Pavloff Harbor would not have been able to survive, as was proved once the mail run converted to air. This was due to the mail boat also providing freight service. In those days, freight meant anything. On our first trip, my father bought three young pigs from a Kodiak resident with the idea of raising our own pork at Perryville. As we headed out of Kodiak from D&A's dock and had just cleared Near Island, the pigs got out of their pen on the upper deck. Everyone was chasing the pigs and managed to catch two, but one of the females jumped off the stern and headed toward the beach, swimming like mad. We always felt she made it as we were pretty close to land. The others were put back in the pen and we made it to Perryville where they caused quite a stir as no one in the village had ever seen a pig. They became regular pets and would follow us like a couple of dogs.

Anyway, the purpose of my letter is to see if you can provide pictures etc. of the old mail boat run and more importantly of Captain Thompson and his boat, the M.V. *Expansion.*

P.S. Our family, except for myself, still all live in Anchorage. My brother Dave started and owns the Ulu Factory in Anchorage.

—*Gaylen R. Gransbury*
12122 NE 162nd Pl.
Bothell, Washington

Starry Nights and Vibrant Days

By Michael V. McGee

EDITOR'S NOTE: *Michael is a freelance writer and former Air Force officer living in North Pole, Alaska. He is author of "An Earthshaking Event, 1964" in Vol. 19, No. 2,* Alaska: The Great Land.

When does an artist achieve fulfillment? When showing paintings in several countries at once and especially having them hang in public buildings all over Japan? When she becomes known in the multidisciplines of painting, sculpture, writing? When she is commissioned by the Marshall Islands to design the first international postage stamps about Alaska? When she has her studio broken into and her paintings stolen for profit? Or is it when she hauls on the rope with a village full of Eskimos to land a beluga whale, helps cut it up, and then retires to her tent to teach the Native children how to draw a whale?

Claire Fejes (pronounced *Feyesh*) would say fulfillment came with living with Eskimos and landing the whale, although all the other definitions also apply to her.

Fejes, now in the sixth decade of her exuberant life, was already known as a sculptor in New York, having studied with renowned sculptors Jose de Creeft and Saul Barzerman of Greenwich Village and having been busily showing on

Claire Fejes came with her husband to Alaska from New York after World War II. When she arrived in the North and saw the sculptures created by some of Alaska's Native artists, she so admired their craftsmanship that she decided to switch to painting, hoping to capture with her watercolors and oils the spirit of the Native way of life. *(Barry McWayne, courtesy of Michael V. McGee)*

57th Avenue, when as a young bride she followed her husband north to Alaska at the end of World War II. Joe had heard of gold near Rampart on the Yukon River, and he was determined to check it out. After a stay in a mining camp, he and Claire settled in Fairbanks where he opened a hobby and art store and became active in the local symphony.

Fejes, the New York sculptor, took one look at the sculpture produced by the Eskimos of Alaska; it was so beautiful she felt she should not compete. "Besides, you cannot chop stone outside when it is 40 below," she says, and she took up painting with watercolors and oils. Fascinated by the Natives, she wanted to live with them and paint them in their natural element. When her two children were old

enough to go to school, she determined to do so, to go live among Eskimos.

Despite her experiences in the mining camp, she was not much of an outdoors woman, so she pitched a tent in her back yard and practiced "camping out." What the neighbors thought of these arrangements is anyone's guess.

Then one day she left her family. She took a small bush plane in 1959 to Kotzebue in northwestern Alaska, then continued her trip in a small, homemade boat across a storm-rough sea to the seasonal Eskimo whaling camp called Sheshalik, nine miles northwest of Kotzebue on the shores of Kotzebue Sound. She was armed with her tent, her sleeping bag, her heavy box of paints and a calm disposition that matched the tranquility of her

hosts, a small group of nomadic hunters and their families.

She joined the corps of women in their duties, cooking, cleaning, cutting up the game and fish, but she also joined the men on the shore watching for beluga whales, waiting for them to come close enough to shore to make hunting possible. The whale meat sustained the villagers through the cold winters, the heavy fat provided the calories to ward off the wind and the plummeting temperatures.

That year the whales did not come while Fejes was there, but another time (she has made six trips), she had better luck. Then she found herself on the end of the rope with seven men and another woman, the rope tied through the beluga's nose as they hauled it ashore. A hunter, with great reverence, poured water over the whale's blowhole, thus assuring the whale of their respect and encouraging its soul to return as another beluga. As the butchering of the whale began, the children couldn't wait to cut off choice pieces of the flippers. Biting into the tough, leathery delicacy, they severed each bite with a swift swipe of the knife between hand and nose. A little girl handed Fejes a piece still warm from the carcass. She chewed on it while contemplating the white whale, the busy Natives and the ocean, planning to repeat the scene in one of her many paintings.

From the journal of her first journey came her first book, *People of the Noatak* (1966), accepted by Alfred A. Knopf Co. on her first try. A similar trip a few years later among the Athabaskan Indians on the Yukon River resulted in another book, *Villagers* (1981), published by Random House. In this book she examined in detail the impact of the white man's civilization on the Indians living a traditional subsistence existence in some of the world's harshest climate. As one bitter hunter complained: "The white man...they shoot the fox and the wolf from the planes, and the trapper that goes with dogs don't have a chance....They have 24 camps around my village." She ends her book with the quote of an Indian woman whom she asks, "Don't Indians ever cry?" She is told, "We were crying, Clara, but you just couldn't see it. The tears were inside."

Fejes has also written a children's book about an Eskimo boy, *Enuk my Son* (1969), and is presently working on her newest book, the story of her early experiences in the state, tentatively called *Cold Starry Nights*, after the name of a painting by Van Gogh.

Her paintings of Indian and Eskimo life hang in 30 museums all over the world and in numerous private collections. "When I paint a portrait, I try to express the inward, not the outward feeling of their lives," Fejes says. On whaling: "The subject fascinates me. I can depict

the land, the animals and the people. Whaling is of vital importance to the people...I have to pick out something of importance to them as well as to me."

Her paintings, with strong emphasis on Native women, have been shown in numerous galleries in America and overseas, including several years with the NIKA group in Japan. Recently, the James Micheners purchased two large paintings for the Arthur M. Huntington Museum at the University of Texas. She has an invitation to show in China, and recently completed the triptych of three paintings to be issued as stamps by the Marshall Islands. Of the 16 paintings stolen from her studio four years ago, six are still missing.

TOP LEFT: This painting is titled "Leela Making Rope Out Of Sealskin." Although she has spent considerable time visiting with Alaska's Natives, artist Claire Fejes draws her inspiration from just being in the North. The mountains, the beauty of the Native people, the light cast by the extreme angle of the sun and the climate have stimulated her to produce impressionistic works, vibrant with bold colors and sculptured forms, which have been called reminiscent of Paul Gauguin and Diego Rivera. *(Courtesy of Claire Fejes)*

BOTTOM LEFT: Claire Fejes' paintings have been displayed worldwide. She has been invited to show in China, and has completed a triptych from which the Marshall Islands have issued a series of commemorative stamps honoring the 30th anniversary of Alaska statehood. *(Michael V. McGee)*

FIRST AMERICANS CAME AT THE END OF THE ICE AGE

New clues from the Far North indicate the first Americans arrived at the end of the Ice Age, some 12,000 years ago, and not before, as some have suggested.

The first hard archaeological evidence supporting the idea that harsh environmental conditions prevented migrations of people from Asia into North America during the Ice Age has been put together by a team of researchers from the University of Alaska Fairbanks and Argonne National Laboratory in Illinois.

The discoveries, made in Alaska's Interior, indicate a close relationship between the oldest sites in the Great Plains and those of the Bering Land Bridge, which connected Asia with the Americas during the Ice Age.

The earliest inhabitants of Alaska manufactured weapons and tools similar to artifacts found at the earliest dated sites, called Paleo-indian, on the plains. Radiocarbon dating places the Alaska sites at no more than a century or two older than the plains sites, suggesting initial New World settlement took place rapidly.

Claims of early sites in the Americas dating from 12,000 to 30,000 years or older have previously been made by many researchers, but without total acceptance by archaeologists. The oldest firmly dated sites in the

This 1989 photo shows an archaeological team excavating along the bluff edge at the Walker Road site. In the background are the Nenana River and Mount Healy (5,716 feet) in the Alaska Range. Pictured from left are Elizabeth Pontti, Jim Foley, Dunrie Greiling, Dana Walukiewicz and Carol Reymiller. *(Courtesy of Ted Goebel)*

Western Hemisphere are no greater than about 11,000 years.

"Harsh environmental

conditions in the Far North prevented earlier migrations from Asia into North America across the Bering Land Bridge," according to University of Alaska Fairbanks graduate John Hoffecker, now with the Argonne National Laboratory, operated by the University of Chicago for the U.S. Department of Energy.

While a 12,000-years-ago date has been thought by some as the time of the first arrival of the first Americans, the recent Alaska discoveries seem, for the first time, to prove the Americas were populated toward the end of the Ice Age.

Until the team's discovery, it appeared that the northernmost regions of the New World were occupied by people whose archaeological remains bore little resemblance to uncovered artifacts in other parts of the New World. Speculation was that a more ancient, and not yet discovered migration must be the source of the oldest known sites in the Great Plains and farther south.

The first evidence for a Paleoindian occupation in Alaska's Interior came from the Dry Creek site, near Healy north of Denali National Park. Excavations during the 1970s led by Roger Powers, head of the university's anthropology department, revealed a small, 11,000-year-old campsite at Dry Creek, nearly 1,000 years older than any other site in Alaska.

"We saw right away that the stone tools from Dry Creek were very much like the similar-aged Paleoindian artifacts found in the plains," said Powers. "But our collection of about 50 artifacts was really too small to prove a connection between late Ice Age hunters in Healy, Alaska and those in, say, Clovis, New Mexico."

In the mid-1980s, Powers' team of archaeologists began work at a site called Walker Road, about five miles north of Healy near the northern boundary of Usibelli Coal Mine. From 1986 through 1990, excavations at Walker Road turned up some 250 stone tools, nearly 10,000 stone flakes, as well as ancient hearths, all radiocarbon dated to about 11,500 years ago.

"Because people were living at Walker Road for longer periods of time, perhaps up to several weeks or even months, we've been able to uncover more of their thrown-away artifacts. The stone tools we've found indicate activities including woodworking, butchering, bone splitting, leather working and possibly clothes making out of hides," said Ted Goebel, University of Alaska Fairbanks doctoral candidate and field supervisor of the Walker Road dig. "Without question the stone tools from Walker Road look very much like Paleoindian stone tools in New Mexico and Arizona." The team also found a dug-out hearth basin for confining a fire, evidence perhaps that the hearth was placed inside a structure. The Walker Road site was inhabited longer than Dry Creek in part because it was a more sheltered location, farther from the Alaska Range and shielded by a ridge from the high winds that sometimes swept the Dry Creek site.

Goebel also says if people had populated Alaska prior to 12,000 years ago, evidence of their existence would have been found by now. He says many archaeologists and geologists have spent their lifetimes searching for clues that humans occupied Alaska during the Ice Age. He also says gold miners in the Interior have overturned tons of earth in search of gold, but all that's been found buried with the metal are ancient fossils of woolly mammoths and other extinct animals, "and there's no indication these wild animals were hunted by humans," Goebel said.

Both Hoffecker, Powers and Goebel say the evidence of people in Alaska at about 12,000 years ago coincides with major environmental changes bringing an end to the Ice Age. They say temperatures in Alaska during the Ice Age weren't warm enough for trees to grow and people weren't able to adapt and survive arctic and subarctic climates. It wasn't until glaciers receded and temperatures rose that prehistoric humans colonized northern Asia and North America, the team concludes.
—*University of Alaska Fairbanks*

Student Kevin Smith records information on the discovery of a stone artifact estimated to be about 10,000 years old during a 1991 excavation at an early man site along Panguingue Creek north of Healy. From these and other excavations, scientists Roger Powers and Ted Goebel of the University of Alaska Fairbanks and John Hoffecker of the Argonne National Laboratory have concluded that early man first came to Alaska about the end of the Ice Age approximately 12,000 years ago. *(Courtesy of Ted Goebel)*

Raven Tales, Traditional Stories of Native Peoples, *edited by Peter Goodchild, Chicago Review Press, Chicago Ill., 1991; 216 pages, 15 black-and-white photos, one map, bibliography and index; softcover, $9.95.*

People have long explained the mysteries of life through storytelling. In this tradition, some of the oldest tales in many cultures have as their central figure the raven. In *Raven Tales*, author Peter Goodchild traces raven myths around the world and through time. He presents variations of raven myths from diverse groups of peoples, such as the Australian aborigines, the ancient Persians and the natives of Siberia. He also speculates on the tales' origins and similarities and how the widespread presence of mythical raven correlates to the growth and migration of civilization.

The most well-developed cycle of raven tales comes from the Tlingit Indians of Southeast Alaska, and Goodchild opens the book with representative Tlingit raven tales. He says the Tlingit tales may form a link with those found in eastern Siberia, where the raven also is the principal mythical figure. Goodchild asks questions such as: "If two tales in two different parts of the world resemble each other, should we say that these tales evolved separately in the two cultures, or are we dealing with a single tale that was brought (or taught) by one culture to the other?"

While raven tales are found primarily among the Tlingit, Haida and Tsimshian Indians of the Northwest coast, the same tales occur in some form among most other tribes of Alaska, the Yukon and western British Columbia. Raven figures appear in mythology of other cultures as well, he writes. In Western tradition, the raven is associated with the Roman god Apollo and the Norse god Odin. The Ainu of Japan, the Malays and

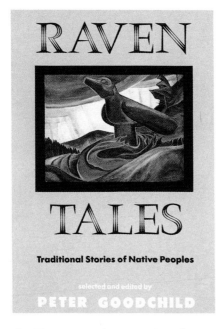

the Vietnamese have stories of a raven or crow that are often tantalizingly similar to those of the raven myths of North America and Siberia.

Goodchild divides the raven stories into "origin" and "trickster" tales. In the origin tales, Raven is a creator, transformer or culture hero that gives people tools, such as fire, needed for survival. In the trickster tales, Raven is a buffoon, liar or thief and acts in a way to provide comic relief. Goodchild suggests that the trickster tales emerged in a North American, New World cycle while the origin tales can be traced to the Old World. Of the origin tales, one of the most important is "The Deluge," a variation on the familiar Noah's ark story. It appears in several Old World cultures. A closely related story is "Earth Diver," a popular Siberian and North American myth about an animal that created dry land by diving into primordial water to bring back mud.

In his attempt to unravel the connections between raven tales, Goodchild broaches a broader topic — the study of myths in general. He introduces a number of theories advanced by other folklore scholars. At some point late in the book, he concludes: "Just as a[n] ... early stone-chopping tool in Africa resembles one from Europe or North America, so the ancient mythical motifs from one continent resemble those of another. The half-human animal figure, the sacred white animal, the intricate solar symbolism, the theft of fire, the identification of the animal symbol with the god, and so on — these are all mythical symbols so old and so diffuse that we can never hope to find their geographic or chronological origins. They entered the New World at some untraceably early date and then emerged as parts of the Raven tales, the Hare tales, the Coyote tales and so on. Nor should we trouble ourselves with the question of whether the

universality of the primeval motifs can be ascribed to the 'similarity of human minds,' or to cultural diffusion; over the course of thousands of years both factors must have been important."

Goodchild's *Raven Tales* may well be, as the book's cover proclaims, "the most complete study of these stories ever published." But Goodchild's writing, with frequent and often cumbersome references to other works on the subject, is sometimes dense and makes the book more an insider's reference than an accessible introduction to raven mythology.

Order from Chicago Review Press, 814 N. Franklin St., Chicago, Ill. 60610.

—L.J. Campbell

Published by
THE ALASKA GEOGRAPHIC SOCIETY

Penny Rennick,
EDITOR

Kathy Doogan,
PRODUCTION DIRECTOR

L.J. Campbell,
STAFF WRITER

Kevin Kerns,
BUSINESS & CIRCULATION MANAGER

Patty Bliss,
CUSTOMER SERVICE REPRESENTATIVE

© 1993 by The Alaska Geographic Society